TypeScript Essentials

Develop large scale responsive web applications
with TypeScript

Christopher Nance

BIRMINGHAM - MUMBAI

TypeScript Essentials

First published: October 2014

Production reference: 1161014

Published by Packt Publishing Ltd.
Livery Place
35 Livery Street
Birmingham B3 2PB, UK.

ISBN 978-1-78398-576-0

www.packtpub.com

Credits

Author

Christopher Nance

Reviewers

Andrea Martinelli

Nathan Rozentals

Basarat Ali Syed

Carlos Ballesteros Velasco

Commissioning Editor

Amarabha Banerjee

Acquisition Editor

Richard Gall

Content Development Editor

Arvind Koul

Technical Editor

Kunal Anil Gaikwad

Copy Editors

Maria Gould

Paul Hindle

Project Coordinator

Neha Bhatnagar

Proofreaders

Simran Bhogal

Ameesha Green

Paul Hindle

Indexers

Monica Ajmera Mehta

Priya Sane

Graphics

Disha Haria

Production Coordinators

Adonia Jones

Komal Ramchandani

Nitesh Thakur

Cover Work

Komal Ramchandani

About the Author

Christopher Nance is an experienced software engineer and has been developing rich web applications for more than 4 years. At KnowledgeLake, he adopted TypeScript to develop a series of reusable components to scale across multiple product offerings and platforms.

I would like to thank my parents for their constant support and encouragement. I would also like to thank my team at KnowledgeLake for pushing me to improve my skills as an engineer.

About the Reviewers

Andrea Martinelli is a passionate software developer who is currently working on Shaman.IO, a tool that automatically detects and extracts structured data from the Web.

In the past, he worked on Songr, a music player and aggregator. His interests span across web data extraction, code performance, and statically typed languages. He is a proficient C# developer and has been interested in TypeScript since its initial announcement. He graduated from the University of Trento in Computer Science and then studied at the Technical University of Denmark, even though he is now dedicating more time to the Shaman.IO project while moving across Europe.

I would like to thank my friends, especially Gianluca and Stefano, for always being supportive. I would also like to thank Prof. Filz, who was one of my most influential teachers in high school. Thanks also to Mads, a special person that I will never forget. And to my family, who I haven't seen for quite a long time.

Nathan Rozentals has been writing commercial software for over 23 years, starting with COBOL on mainframes, through C, on to C++ and Java, and finally settling on C# and ASP.NET.

He picked up TypeScript in October 2012 — a day after the 0.8.0 release — and could not put it down. In TypeScript, he found a language that could bring all of the design patterns and practices he had learned over the years — in a variety of languages — to JavaScript.

Some 6 days after the 0.8.0 release, he began blogging about TypeScript; covering a variety of topics, including unit testing, implementing an IoC container, and organizing code with AMD modules. He knew he had hit the mark when Microsoft themselves started to reference his blog in their CodePlex discussion forums.

You can find his blog at `http://blorkfish.wordpress.com`.

He currently works in the health industry, bringing touchscreen interfaces to medical systems, thereby enabling BYOD for clinicians and hospital staff.

He is passionate about code quality, unit testing, and continuous integration, and has helped many large teams implement CI across many different software projects in many different languages.

When he is not coding, he loves windsurfing and playing soccer. He is also an avid Liverpool FC supporter.

> I would like to thank my partner, Kathy, for her never ending love and support, and for giving me the freedom to spend long hours working on something that I am so passionate about. You are the best.
>
> To Ayron and Dayna — you are always in my thoughts — your enthusiasm for life and curious nature have given me such inspiration. I will always be there for you.

Basarat Ali Syed (BAS) is a senior developer and the go-to guy for frontend issues at Picnic Software (`http://picnicsoftware.com/`) in Melbourne, Australia. He has a Master of Computing degree from Australian National University and graduated with high distinction in all courses. He is a familiar face at developer meetups and conferences in Australia and has been a speaker at events such as ALT.NET, DDD Melbourne, MelbJS, and Node.js meetups, among others. He is deeply passionate about web technologies. He is a known member of the TypeScript community and works on the DefinitelyTyped team (`https://github.com/DefinitelyTyped`). In his spare time, he enjoys bodybuilding, cycling, and maintains a YouTube channel for helping fellow developers (`http://youtube.com/basaratali`). You can easily find him on Twitter @basarat, `www.github.com/basarat`, and `www.basarat.com`.

www.PacktPub.com

Support files, eBooks, discount offers, and more

For support files and downloads related to your book, please visit www.PacktPub.com.

Did you know that Packt offers eBook versions of every book published, with PDF and ePub files available? You can upgrade to the eBook version at www.PacktPub.com and as a print book customer, you are entitled to a discount on the eBook copy. Get in touch with us at service@packtpub.com for more details.

At www.PacktPub.com, you can also read a collection of free technical articles, sign up for a range of free newsletters and receive exclusive discounts and offers on Packt books and eBooks.

http://PacktLib.PacktPub.com

Do you need instant solutions to your IT questions? PacktLib is Packt's online digital book library. Here, you can search, access, and read Packt's entire library of books.

Why subscribe?

- Fully searchable across every book published by Packt
- Copy and paste, print, and bookmark content
- On demand and accessible via a web browser

Free access for Packt account holders

If you have an account with Packt at www.PacktPub.com, you can use this to access PacktLib today and view nine entirely free books. Simply use your login credentials for immediate access.

Table of Contents

Preface

This book is a quick and useful guide to learning the TypeScript language. The language features that TypeScript provides on top of JavaScript are covered thoroughly in this book with hands-on examples. TypeScript is a fairly new development language that can ease the pain of normal JavaScript development. Starting from downloading the compiler, covering language features, and implementing a dynamic application, this book will leave you ready to create new, large-scale JavaScript-based applications.

What this book covers

Chapter 1, *Getting Started with TypeScript*, covers setting up an environment for developing TypeScript applications and creating a simple application.

Chapter 2, *TypeScript Basics*, covers the primary language features that TypeScript creates on top of JavaScript and how each of these features compiles into plain JavaScript.

Chapter 3, *The TypeScript Compiler*, examines the TypeScript compiler and the different parameters that it accepts. The results of the different parameters will be discussed as well as how they affect the final JavaScript output.

Chapter 4, *Object-oriented Programming with TypeScript*, is all about the basics of object-oriented programming. You will be presented with the benefits that TypeScript adds to make ECMA Script a more full-fledged object-oriented language.

Chapter 5, *Creating a Simple Drawing Application*, walks you through creating a simple drawing application using the concepts already covered in the book. By the end of the chapter, you will have created a web-based drawing application that will give you a good understanding of writing complex applications using TypeScript.

Chapter 6, Declaration Files and Library Integrations, discusses declaration files and how they help us integrate with other JavaScript libraries. Libraries such as jQuery, KnockoutJS, and RequireJS will be covered.

Chapter 7, Enhancing the Drawing Application, re-examines the drawing application and shows you how to create a more reusable set of objects. Module definitions will be created and the process of minifying code is covered.

Chapter 8, Debugging TypeScript, discusses the different options available to debug TypeScript once it is deployed and running. We also cover unit testing and test-driven development, which will allow us to test functionality with code.

What you need for this book

TypeScript has a standalone compiler install, so any text editor can be used to develop TypeScript applications. The examples provided with this book will use Microsoft's Visual Studio, and it is recommended that you use it too to help you follow the examples; however, this is not a requirement. A basic understanding of JavaScript and web development is required as not every language construct will be covered; just the ones that TypeScript provides on top of it.

Who this book is for

This book is intended to introduce the TypeScript language and its features to anyone looking to develop rich web applications. Whether you are new to web development or are an experienced engineer with strong JavaScript skills, this book will get you writing code quickly. A basic understanding of JavaScript and its language features is necessary for this book.

Conventions

In this book, you will find a number of styles of text that distinguish between different kinds of information. Here are some examples of these styles, and an explanation of their meaning.

Code words in text, database table names, folder names, filenames, file extensions, pathnames, dummy URLs, user input, and Twitter handles are shown as follows: "To get started, let's create a new file on the filesystem and call it `HelloWorld.ts`."

A block of code is set as follows:

```
var p = document.createElement('p');
var hello: string = "Hello";
var world: string = 2;
p.textContent = hello + " " + world;

document.body.appendChild(p);
```

Any command-line input or output is written as follows:

```
tsc HelloWorld.ts
```

New terms and **important words** are shown in bold. Words that you see on the screen, in menus or dialog boxes for example, appear in the text like this: "To create a new project that includes TypeScript, go to the **File** menu and navigate to **New | Project**."

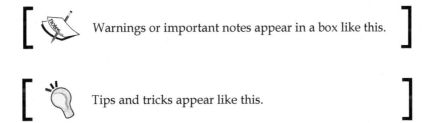

> Warnings or important notes appear in a box like this.

> Tips and tricks appear like this.

Reader feedback

Feedback from our readers is always welcome. Let us know what you think about this book—what you liked or may have disliked. Reader feedback is important for us to develop titles that you really get the most out of.

To send us general feedback, simply send an e-mail to feedback@packtpub.com, and mention the book title via the subject of your message.

If there is a topic that you have expertise in and you are interested in either writing or contributing to a book, see our author guide on www.packtpub.com/authors.

Customer support

Now that you are the proud owner of a Packt book, we have a number of things to help you to get the most from your purchase.

Downloading the example code

You can download the example code files for all Packt books you have purchased from your account at http://www.packtpub.com. If you purchased this book elsewhere, you can visit http://www.packtpub.com/support and register to have the files e-mailed directly to you.

Errata

Although we have taken every care to ensure the accuracy of our content, mistakes do happen. If you find a mistake in one of our books—maybe a mistake in the text or the code—we would be grateful if you would report this to us. By doing so, you can save other readers from frustration and help us improve subsequent versions of this book. If you find any errata, please report them by visiting http://www.packtpub.com/submit-errata, selecting your book, clicking on the **errata submission form** link, and entering the details of your errata. Once your errata are verified, your submission will be accepted and the errata will be uploaded on our website, or added to any list of existing errata, under the Errata section of that title. Any existing errata can be viewed by selecting your title from http://www.packtpub.com/support.

Piracy

Piracy of copyright material on the Internet is an ongoing problem across all media. At Packt, we take the protection of our copyright and licenses very seriously. If you come across any illegal copies of our works, in any form, on the Internet, please provide us with the location address or website name immediately so that we can pursue a remedy.

Please contact us at copyright@packtpub.com with a link to the suspected pirated material.

We appreciate your help in protecting our authors, and our ability to bring you valuable content.

Questions

You can contact us at questions@packtpub.com if you are having a problem with any aspect of the book, and we will do our best to address it.

1
Getting Started with TypeScript

There are many languages available that can be used to create cross-platform applications and these types of code applications are being created daily. Some of the more common languages that these applications use are Java, C, and JavaScript and each has its advantages and disadvantages. While JavaScript is easy to get started with, it is also easy to lose control of. C requires a lot of overhead to create complex applications such as memory management, and Java requires the Java runtime to be installed. As applications grow and become more complex, so does the need to produce maintainable code. TypeScript is a new open source language created to make web development easier and more reliable. In this chapter we will:

- Understand what TypeScript is
- Learn how TypeScript improves on the foundations of JavaScript
- Explore the ways TypeScript makes code more maintainable
- Learn how to get the TypeScript compiler
- Create our first application in TypeScript

The advantages of TypeScript

As hardware technology has advanced, so too has the need for more advanced software applications to run not just on one device but on an array of devices. JavaScript is the natural solution to this cross-platform model since almost all modern browsers are capable of running it. Unfortunately, the development paradigm of JavaScript is still dependent upon complex pattern knowledge, and debugging must be done at runtime. Creating large applications in JavaScript can be difficult and structuring the code in a maintainable form is just as difficult. TypeScript, an open source language project started by Microsoft, aims to take JavaScript development to the next level.

JavaScript originally ran as an interpreted language and still does in some places, while modern browsers convert it to machine code during execution. What this means is that the code you write is the code being used at runtime. The advantage of using interpreted languages is that they provide a rapid development model with very little overhead for the developer. They work in cross-platform environments because the code does not need to be compiled for each new device it is deployed to. Interpreted languages aren't without their share of disadvantages either though. In most modern implementations, JavaScript code must be run through a just-in-time compiler first, but even with the help of this compilation, the dynamic typing of the language makes this a difficult task and performance can suffer. On top of the performance hit, JavaScript code must still be deployed before testing can be done. A single syntax error will force you to run the application, track down the source of the problem, fix it, and then run the application again, which wastes a lot of time and can be quite frustrating. Developers like to refactor code as better ways to solve problems arise or new functionality is needed. This refactoring could cause other parts of the application to fail and without performing complete regression testing the problem could be overlooked. To interact with an object you must have intimate knowledge of the type that the object represents. TypeScript aims to solve these problems through a variety of additions to the JavaScript language including a compilation step with a detailed list of errors.

TypeScript is a statically typed compiled language that generates JavaScript code that can be used in cross-platform scenarios. You may be thinking to yourself at this point: why would I want to rewrite all of the applications I already have in this new language? The simple answer is you don't have to. TypeScript is just a superset of JavaScript that gets compiled into plain JavaScript. Although almost all of your existing JavaScript code is valid TypeScript code, certain pieces will need to be adapted to ensure safe compilation; however, they will generally improve the quality of your code. You are free to type your code as strong or as weak as you wish but I highly recommend embracing the typing system completely.

JavaScript was originally created as a scripting language, but as the need for larger applications has grown so has the need for those applications to contain more reusable components and libraries. JavaScript is dynamic enough to act as both a functional language and an object-oriented one through certain design patterns. Object-oriented code is focused on the concept of code reuse and we will be investigating it during our journey into TypeScript. TypeScript provides a rich set of object types and accessibility levels that will seem very familiar to object-oriented developers. Inheritance, encapsulation, and abstraction are all made easier in TypeScript. JavaScript is focused on the value of functions and prototype-based inheritance, which means TypeScript is as well. This can seem strange to anyone used to the idea of class-based inheritance. So through the use of its compiler, TypeScript introduces a number of important concepts from a few different object-oriented languages. These are as follows:

- Static typing
- Classes
- Interfaces
- Generics
- Modules

TypeScript adds a static typing layer on top of JavaScript that is then run through a compiler. The compiler parses the TypeScript code and converts it into plain JavaScript. The addition of type safety and code compilation allows errors to be caught sooner and bugs to be eliminated without ever having to deploy a line of code. The introduction of classes and modules makes the development of large scale applications much easier. Including generics and interfaces in the type system allows us to easily create components and libraries that can be used with a variety of objects.

On top of this, TypeScript introduces the idea of public and private members. If an object or function attempts to access a private member of another object the compiler will recognize that the code is invalid and a build error will be generated. This helps implement encapsulation, which is meant to prevent consumers of your TypeScript objects from accessing methods and properties that could be potentially harmful when manipulated outside of the scope of the object itself. Providing accessibility levels helps us limit the scope of possible interactions with an object or even hide it completely from access by other components or libraries.

 Keep in mind that the output from the compiler is just JavaScript code and when it is run, any segment of code that has access to the object can manipulate any property of the object.

Writing unit tests has become common practice in software development. Unit tests allow us as developers to refactor and clean code with the safety of knowing that we are not breaking existing functionality. The design decision to include interfaces in the language specification for TypeScript has helped to improve the testability of our code. Writing unit tests help us to verify that small segmented blocks of code always operate as expected. However, as our applications grow we must pass around more complex objects and create more complex functions. This makes testing small segments of code individually more difficult. With the addition of interfaces, it is now easier to mock up objects to be passed around and more tightly control the scope of the tests.

Another key component of JavaScript development is the ability to integrate third-party libraries. It is difficult to find rich web applications these days that don't integrate with jQuery, which has advantages and disadvantages. Due to the open nature of JavaScript development, libraries exist to do almost anything and a lot of them are free to use. Later on we will discuss how TypeScript is already equipped to integrate with these libraries and make the development experience infinitely better. For now, let's focus on getting ready to write our first application in TypeScript.

Setting up the IDE

To start writing code in TypeScript, we first need to install the compiler. The compiler is available as a standalone package through Node.js, Visual Studio tooling that Microsoft provides, or you can directly download the compiler's source code. Throughout this text we will be using Visual Studio 2013 as our interactive development environment (IDE). Visual Studio 2013 provides native support for TypeScript with the release of Update 2. For Visual Studio 2012, Microsoft provides an extension that can be installed from the TypeScript home page (`http://www.typescriptlang.org/`). As TypeScript is becoming more widespread, the number of code editors that have support for it has grown including Eclipse (`http://www.jetbrains.com/webstorm/`) and Notepad++ (`https://github.com/hansrwindhoff/nppPluginTypescript`).

The TypeScript compiler, as with a number of modern languages, is written in TypeScript, which means it will compile to plain JavaScript and run in any JavaScript host. With Microsoft's tools installed, you can access the TypeScript compiler directly from the command line and generate JavaScript immediately. The following screenshot shows a list of the available compiler options and what they do. We will look at each of these options more thoroughly later on but for now you can see that the compiler, although very new, already has a very robust feature set

```
C:\>tsc
Version 1.0.0.0
Syntax:   tsc [options] [file ..]

Examples: tsc hello.ts
          tsc --out foo.js foo.ts
          tsc @args.txt

Options:
  --codepage NUMBER              Specify the codepage to use when opening source
files.
  -d, --declaration              Generates corresponding .d.ts file.
  -h, --help                     Print this message.
  --mapRoot LOCATION             Specifies the location where debugger should loc
ate map files instead of generated locations.
  -m KIND, --module KIND         Specify module code generation: 'commonjs' or 'a
md'
  --noImplicitAny                Warn on expressions and declarations with an imp
lied 'any' type.
  --out FILE                     Concatenate and emit output to single file.
  --outDir DIRECTORY             Redirect output structure to the directory.
  --removeComments               Do not emit comments to output.
  --sourcemap                    Generates corresponding .map file.
  --sourceRoot LOCATION          Specifies the location where debugger should loc
ate TypeScript files instead of source locations.
  -t VERSION, --target VERSION   Specify ECMAScript target version: 'ES3' (defaul
t), or 'ES5'
  -v, --version                  Print the compiler's version: 1.0.0.0
  @<file>                        Insert command line options and files from a fil
e.
```

As you can see the list of options is fairly extensive so far and will undoubtedly become richer as the language develops. TypeScript 1.0, which will be the version of the language used in this text, provides parameters for everything from specifying the output file to warnings based on code rules. We will discuss all of these options later on, but for now all you need to know is that you can compile your TypeScript code by passing the compiler the path of the file you want to compile. When we begin to build more complicated applications the Visual Studio integrations will provide an easy way for you to set compiler options for all TypeScript files included in your projects.

Hello World

Now that we have the compiler installed, let's start writing some code. This wouldn't be a good technical book without the inclusion of "Hello World" to get you started with writing code in a new language. The code for this particular example is pretty simple, but we can use it to demonstrate some of the early benefits of switching to TypeScript.

Command-line compilation

The TypeScript compiler is nothing more than JavaScript code; it is possible to compile your TypeScript anywhere that a JavaScript host exists. Earlier, we saw that an executable was provided that allows us to compile our code from the command line. We will walk through this first example using this executable and discover how simple it is to get going with TypeScript. To get started, let's create a new file on the filesystem and call it `HelloWorld.ts`. The following code creates a new HTML paragraph element and sets the text to the value of a pair strings concatenated together:

```
var p = document.createElement('p');
var hello: string = "Hello";
var world: string = 2;
p.textContent = hello + " " + world;

document.body.appendChild(p);
```

For the most part, this looks like plain old JavaScript. However, if you pay close attention to the declaration of the `hello` and `world` variables, you will see something new. After the variable names, you will see that they are now given the type of `string`. This type annotation tells the compiler to always treat the variables `hello` and `world` as strings; however, in this case, the compiler can infer these types from their initial values. Every other reference to these variables will be able to assume that all of the properties and methods of an object of the type `string` will be accessible. This allows IDEs to provide intelligent code completion as well as visually alert us if we are performing an action that the compiler is going to fail on. Now let's verify that this code compiles and analyze the JavaScript that the compiler outputs.

> **Downloading the example code**
>
> You can download the example code files for all Packt books you have purchased from your account at http://www.packtpub.com. If you purchased this book elsewhere, you can visit http://www.packtpub.com/support and register to have the files e-mailed directly to you.

Launch an instance of the command prompt and browse to the directory where you created the `HelloWorld.ts` file. From here, running the compiler is as simple as typing the following:

```
tsc HelloWorld.ts
```

This generates the following output:

```
C:\HelloWorld>tsc HelloWorld.ts
C:/HelloWorld/HelloWorld.ts(5,1): error TS2011: Cannot convert 'number' to 'string'.
```

As you can see, the compiler recognizes that we typed the `world` variable as `string` and then tried to assign a numeric value to it. While that would have been legal JavaScript, it could lead to data errors later when another piece of code is expecting `world` to be `string`. So let's go back to the TypeScript file and modify the value we are assigning to `world` and run the compiler again:

```typescript
var world: string = "World!";
```

Success! Our code has successfully made it through the TypeScript compiler and it generated a JavaScript file by the name of `HelloWorld.js`. If you open up this file, you will find the resulting code that will be deployed and run on the client. As you can see, the type annotations were stripped out of the final code, while maintaining a one-to-one mapping between our TypeScript code and the resulting JavaScript code, because they are not actually part of the JavaScript language specification:

```javascript
    var p = document.createElement('p');
var hello = "Hello";
var world = "World!";
p.textContent = hello + " " + world;

document.body.appendChild(p);
```

Now that we have our JavaScript generated, we need to test it. The first thing our code is attempting to do is to create a new HTML paragraph element. So we will need to generate an HTML file to load our code and be available for manipulation. Then two parts of a message are concatenated together and assigned to the text value of the paragraph element that has just been created. Finally, the paragraph element is appended to the body of the HTML document. The following HTML code will load our generated JavaScript file:

```html
<html>
<head>
    <title>Hello World</title>
</head>
```

```
<body>
    <script src="HelloWorld.js" ></script>
</body>
</html>
```

 In general, script tags should be included within the `<head>` tag, not in the main `<body>` tag. In this case, our code is dependent upon the DOM being ready for our code to execute successfully.

Opening the HTML file in a browser will result in the immediate execution of our code when the document's body loads. As you can see in the following screenshot, our paragraph was added to the HTML on the page and **Hello World!** is displayed:

So as you can see, creating and compiling TypeScript applications is just as easy as creating a basic JavaScript application. However, running the compiler from the command line will become cumbersome as the applications you develop grow in size and complexity. So let's go over setting up a TypeScript project in Visual Studio and get the Hello World application running in a web-based project.

Integrating Visual Studio

Now that we have created a simple application and discovered how TypeScript generates JavaScript that can be deployed, let's cover the integration with Visual Studio or Visual Studio Express, which is a free version of Visual Studio available at `http://www.visualstudio.com/en-us/products/visual-studio-express-vs.aspx`. Once you have the Visual Studio tooling installed for TypeScript, you will be able to create new projects that are set up to use our new language of choice.

Creating a new project

To create a new project that includes TypeScript, go to the **File** menu and navigate to **New | Project**. In the **New Project** window, you will see a list of installed templates. There is now a new section named **TypeScript**; select this section and you will see all of the available project templates that can be used to create TypeScript applications.

 The location of this template may vary depending on the version of Visual Studio installed. If the TypeScript section is not available, use the search function of the project template selector.

This does not mean that TypeScript can only be added to these project types—you can add TypeScript files to any existing project. For our examples, we will be using the **HTML Application with TypeScript** project template, so let's select that and create our new application:

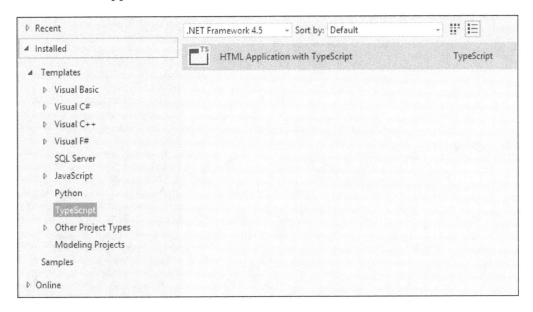

Once the project has been created you will notice a few things right away. First, a default TypeScript file and HTML file have been created to host our new application. There is also a `web.config` and CSS file to host your application styles. All of these elements should seem pretty familiar to you, except the TypeScript file, which is there in place of a JavaScript file.

Now that our project has been created we need to move our code in. Copy the code from `HelloWorld.ts` into `app.ts` and do the same with the HTML that was generated. Change the script tag's source attribute to `app.js` to reference the new location of our code and run the application. The output displayed should be the same.

Build options

Visual Studio has provided a seamless integration with TypeScript and provides a large variety of configuration options. Let's take a look at the project build options first and get a feel for the different things that TypeScript can generate when it is being compiled. To find the build options, right-click on the project in the solution explorer and select **Properties** from the context menu. As you can see in the following screenshot, we are able to manipulate a large number of the compiler options we saw earlier:

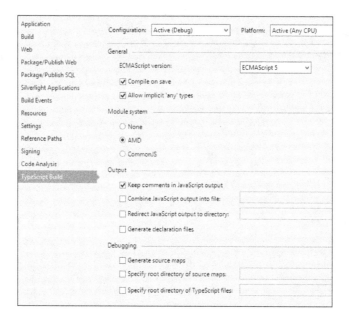

From the build settings you can see that we have the ability to change which version of JavaScript we want to compile our TypeScript into: ECMAScript 5 or ECMAScript 3.

 JavaScript is now formally known as ECMAScript but it is still commonly referred to as its original name.

You also have the option for compiling TypeScript files when you save changes to them. This is a helpful option because when a TypeScript file is compiled so are all other TypeScript files that it references. This is a helpful feature when you have only a few files being referenced, but as your applications grow and the dependency trees become more complex you could run into performance issues. Allowing implicit "any" types tells the compiler not to fail if an object's type is not given or cannot be implied. Unchecking this option is the easiest way to force yourself to fully embrace the type system. Although you may run across some scenarios where an "any" type is inevitable they should be very rare. This can be done by providing a type annotation as shown here:

```
var explicitAny: any;
```

We also have the ability to change the module system we want to use when our JavaScript code is generated. We will discuss modules and the differences between each of our available options later on, but it is important to be aware of this option because it could drastically change the way our final code looks.

The output section gives us a variety of options for what the final output from the compiler will be. Commenting code is a very useful way of making it maintainable, but this can bloat the size of a JavaScript file. This could cause performance problems when downloading the code to a remote client over the web. Since Visual Studio gives us the ability to define different compiler options for different build configurations, we could allow the comments to remain in the output for debugging while removing them for release builds. The **Combine JavaScript output into file** option allows us to combine all of our generated code into a single output file. This becomes incredibly useful as the number of files in our project grows and there are a lot of network calls taking place to get each file one at a time.

We also have the ability to change the output path of the generated JavaScript. This gives us the ability to push changes directly into a test environment upon successful compilation without ever having to bring down the site or manually copy files to the deployment location. The last option in the output section is a very interesting one. Checking the **Generate declaration files** option will create declaration files for each of the types you create. These declaration files can then be referenced by other TypeScript files to provide a type definition for objects of a specific type. We will discuss declaration files in more depth later on in the book.

The final section is related to how we want to debug our TypeScript code. We have the ability to generate source maps and the directory in which they should be deployed to. Source maps provide a way for debugging combined and minified JavaScript code. They are particularly helpful when debugging code that has been pushed into production by creating a way to make the JavaScript readable, however, in TypeScript they also provide us with a way back to the original TypeScript code. The final option specifies where the TypeScript files are located; this will allow debugging from inside of Visual Studio directly. In most scenarios, the default option here will suffice.

Summary

The things learned in this chapter will be the basis for continuing our journey into TypeScript. We have discussed a variety of ways in which TypeScript improves the JavaScript development model. TypeScript makes large scale application development easier with the addition of a static typing system and code completion. Visual Studio's intellisense feature brings JavaScript development in line with other languages such as C# and Visual Basic. We briefly discussed the compiler and how it turns TypeScript into deployable JavaScript and created our first application. All of the examples shown moving forward will be using Visual Studio; however, feel free to use your favorite IDE. In the next chapter, we will discuss the different language features provided by TypeScript and how the compiler generates its JavaScript output.

2
TypeScript Basics

One of the primary benefits of compiled languages is that they provide a more plain syntax for the developer to work with before the code is eventually converted to machine code. TypeScript is able to bring this advantage to JavaScript development by wrapping several different patterns into language constructs that allow us to write better code. We have talked a little bit about the static type system that TypeScript adds on top of JavaScript. Every explicit type annotation that is provided is simply syntactic sugar that will be removed during compilation, but not before their constraints are analyzed and any errors are caught. In this chapter, we will explore this type system in depth. We will also discuss the different language structures that TypeScript introduces. We will look at how these structures are emitted by the compiler into plain JavaScript. This chapter will contain a detailed look at each of these concepts:

- Types
- Functions
- Interfaces
- Classes
- Enums
- Modules
- Generic types

Types

In *Chapter 1, Getting Started with TypeScript,* we wrote our first TypeScript application and briefly glanced at the static type system. Two variables were created and were given static type annotations to declare them as string objects. These type annotations put a specific set of constraints on the variables being created. These constraints allow the compiler and development tools to better assist in the proper use of the object. This includes a list of functions, variables, and properties available on the object. If a variable is created and no type is provided for it, TypeScript will attempt to infer the type from the context in which it is used. For instance, in the following code, we do not explicitly declare the variable `hello` as `string`; however, since it is created with an initial value, TypeScript is able to infer that it should always be treated as a string:

```
var hello = "Hello There";
```

The ability of TypeScript to do this contextual typing provides development tools with the ability to enhance the development experience in a variety of ways. The type information allows our IDE to warn us of potential errors in our code, or provide intelligent code completion and suggestion. As you can see from the following screenshot, Visual Studio is able to provide a list of methods and properties associated with string objects as well as their type information:

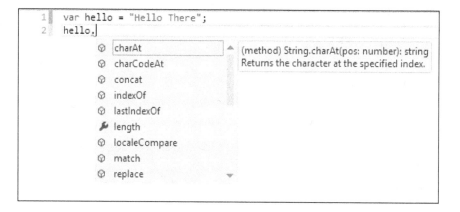

When an object's type is not given and cannot be inferred from its initialization then it will be treated as an `Any` type. The Any type is the base type for all other types in TypeScript. It can represent any JavaScript value and the minimum amount of type checking is performed on objects of type `Any`. Every other type that exists in TypeScript falls into one of three categories: primitive types, object types, or type parameters. TypeScript's primitive types closely mirror those of JavaScript.

The TypeScript primitive types are as follows:

- **Number**: `var myNum: number = 2;`
- **Boolean**: `var myBool: boolean = true;`
- **String**: `var myString: string = "Hello";`
- **Void**: `function(): void { var x = 2; }`
- **Null**: `if (x != null) { alert(x); }`
- **Undefined**: `if (x != undefined) { alert(x); }`

All of these types correspond directly to JavaScript's primitive types except for `Void`. The `Void` type is meant to represent the absence of a value. A function that returns no value has a return type of void. Object types are the most common types you will see in TypeScript and they are made up of references to classes, interfaces, and anonymous object types. Object types are made up of a complex set of members. These members fall into one of four categories: properties, call signatures, constructor signatures, or index signatures. Later in this chapter, we will start creating different object types using the different language entities in TypeScript.

Type parameters are used when referencing generic types or calling generic functions. Type parameters are used to keep code generic enough to be used on a multitude of objects while limiting those objects to a specific set of constraints. An early example of generics that we can cover is arrays. Arrays exist just like they do in JavaScript and they have an extra set of type constraints placed upon them. The `array` object itself has certain type constraints and methods that are created as being an object of the `Array` type, the second piece of information that comes from the array declaration is the type of the objects contained in the array. There are two ways to explicitly type an array; otherwise, the contextual typing system will attempt to infer the type information:

```
var array1: string[] = [];
var array2: Array<string> = [];
```

Both of these examples are completely legal ways of declaring an array. They both generate the same JavaScript output and they both provide the same type information. The first example is a shorthand type literal using the [and] characters to create arrays. The resulting JavaScript for each of these arrays is shown as follows:

```
var array1 = [];
var array2 = [];
```

Despite all of the type annotations and compile-time checking, TypeScript compiles to plain JavaScript and therefore adds absolutely no overhead to the run time speed of your applications. All of the type annotations are removed from the final code, providing us with both a much richer development experience and a clean finished product.

Functions

If you are at all familiar with JavaScript you will be very familiar with the concept of functions. TypeScript has added type annotations to the parameter list as well as the return type. Due to the new constraints being placed on the parameter list, the concept of function overloads was also included in the language specification. TypeScript also takes advantage of JavaScript's **arguments** object and provides syntax for rest parameters. Let's take a look at a function declaration in TypeScript:

```
function add(x: number, y: number): number {
    return x + y;
}
```

As you can see, we have created a function called add. It takes two parameters that are both of the type number, one of the primitive types, and it returns a number. This function is useful in its current form but it is a little limited in overall functionality. What if we want to add a third number to the first two? Then we have to call our function multiple times. TypeScript provides a way to provide optional parameters to functions. So now we can modify our function to take a third parameter, z, that will get added to the first two numbers, as shown in the following code:

```
function add(x: number, y: number, z?: number) {
    if (z !== undefined) {
        return x + y + z;
    }
    return x + y;
}
```

As you can see, we have a third named parameter now but this one is followed by ?. This tells the compiler that this parameter is not required for the function to be called.

Optional parameters tell the compiler not to generate an error if the parameter is not provided when the function is called. In JavaScript, this compile-time checking is not performed, meaning an exception could occur at runtime because each missing parameter will have a value of undefined. It is the responsibility of the developer to write code that verifies a value exists before attempting to use it.

So now we can add three numbers together and we haven't broken any of our previous code that relied on the add method only taking two parameters. This has added a little bit more functionality but I think it would be nice to extend this code to operate on multiple types. We know that strings can be added together just the same as numbers can, so why not use the same method? In its current form, though, passing strings to the add function will result in compilation errors. We will modify the function's definition to take not only numbers but strings as well, as shown in the following code:

```
function add(x: string, y: string): string;
function add(x: number, y: number): number;
function add(x: any, y: any): any {
    return x + y;
}
```

As you can see, we now have two declarations of the add function: one for strings, one for numbers, and then we have the final implementation using the any type. The signature of the actual function implementation is not included in the function's type definition, though. Attempting to call our add method with anything other than a number or string will fail at compile time, however, the overloads have no effect on the generated JavaScript. All of the type annotations are stripped out, as well as the overloads, and all we are left with is a very simple JavaScript method:

```
function add(x, y) {
    return x + y;
}
```

Great, so now we have a multipurpose add function that can take two values and combine them together for either strings or numbers. This still feels a little limited in overall functionality though. What if we wanted to add an indeterminate number of values together? We would have to call our add method over and over again until we eventually had only one value. Thankfully, TypeScript includes rest parameters, which is essentially an unbounded list of optional parameters.

The following code shows how to modify our add functions to include a rest parameter:

```
function add(arg1: string, ...args: string[]): string;
function add(arg1: number, ...args: number[]): number;
function add(arg1: any, ...args: any[]): any {
    var total = arg1;
    for (var i = 0; i < args.length; i++) {
        total += args[i];
    }
    return total;
}
```

A rest parameter can only be the final parameter in a function's declaration. The TypeScript compiler recognizes the syntax of this final parameter and generates an extra bit of JavaScript to generate a shifted array from the JavaScript `arguments` object that is available to code inside of a function. The resulting JavaScript code shows the loop that the compiler has added to create the array that represents our indeterminate list of parameters:

```
function add(arg1) {
    var args = [];
    for (var _i = 0; _i < (arguments.length - 1); _i++) {
        args[_i] = arguments[_i + 1];
    }
    var total = arg1;
    for (var i = 0; i < args.length; i++) {
        total += args[i];
    }
    return total;
}
```

Now adding numbers and strings together is very simple and is completely type-safe. If you attempt to mix the different parameter types, a compile error will occur. The first two of the following statements are legal calls to our Add function; however, the third is not because the objects being passed in are not of the same type:

```
alert(add("Hello ", "World!"));
alert(add(3, 5, 9, 120, 42));
//Error
alert(add(3, "World!"));
```

We are still very early into our exploration of TypeScript but the benefits are already very apparent. There are still a few features of functions that we haven't covered yet but we need to learn more about the language first. Next, we will discuss the interface construct and the benefits it provides with absolutely no cost.

Interfaces

Interfaces are a key piece of creating large-scale software applications. They are a way of representing complex types about any object. Despite their usefulness they have absolutely no runtime consequences because JavaScript does not include any sort of runtime type checking. Interfaces are analyzed at compile time and then omitted from the resulting JavaScript. Interfaces create a contract for developers to use when developing new objects or writing methods to interact with existing ones. Interfaces are named types that contain a list of members. Let's look at an example of an interface:

```
interface IPoint {
    x: number;
    y: number;
}
```

As you can see we use the `interface` keyword to start the interface declaration. Then we give the interface a name that we can easily reference from our code.

 Interfaces can be named anything, for example, foo or bar, however, a simple naming convention will improve the readability of the code. Throughout this book, interfaces will be given the format I<name> and object types will just use <name>, for example, IFoo and Foo.

The interfaces' declaration body contains just a list of members and functions and their types. Interface members can only be instance members of an object. Using the static keyword in an interface declaration will result in a compile error.

Interfaces have the ability to inherit from base types. This interface inheritance allows us to extend existing interfaces into a more enhanced version as well as merge separate interfaces together. To create an inheritance chain, interfaces use the `extends` clause. The `extends` clause is followed by a comma-separated list of types that the interface will merge with.

```
interface IAdder {
    add(arg1: number, ...args: number[]): number;
}
interface ISubtractor {
    subtract(arg1: number, ...args: number[]): number;
}
interface ICalculator extends IAdder, ISubtractor {
    multiply(arg1: number, ...args: number[]): number;
    divide(arg1: number, arg2: number): number;
}
```

Here, we see three interfaces:

- `IAdder`, which defines a type that must implement the `add` method that we wrote earlier
- `ISubtractor`, which defines a new method called `subtract` that any object typed with `ISubtractor` must define
- `ICalculator`, which extends both `IAdder` and `ISubtractor` as well as defining two new methods that perform operations a calculator would be responsible for, which an adder or subtractor wouldn't perform

These interfaces can now be referenced in our code as type parameters or type declarations. Interfaces cannot be directly instantiated and attempting to reference the members of an interface by using its type name directly will result in an error. In the following function declaration the `ICalculator` interface is used to restrict the object type that can be passed to the function. The compiler can now examine the function body and infer all of the type information associated with the calculator parameter and warn us if the object used does not implement this interface.

```
function performCalculations(calculator: ICalculator, num1, num2) {
    calculator.add(num1, num2);
    calculator.subtract(num1, num2);
    calculator.multiply(num1, num2);
    calculator.divide(num1, num2);
    return true;
}
```

The last thing that you need to know about interface definitions is that their declarations are open-ended and will implicitly merge together if they have the same type name. Our `ICalculator` interface could have been split into two separate declarations with each one adding its own list of base types and its own list of members. The resulting type definition from the following declaration is equivalent to the declaration we saw previously:

```
interface ICalculator extends IAdder {
    multiply(arg1: number, ...args: number[]): number;
}
interface ICalculator extends ISubtractor {
    divide(arg1: number, arg2: number): number;
}
```

Creating large scale applications requires code that is flexible and reusable. Interfaces are a key component of keeping TypeScript as flexible as plain JavaScript, yet allow us to take advantage of the type checking provided at compile time. Your code doesn't have to be dependent on existing object types and will be ready for any new object types that might be introduced. The TypeScript compiler also implements a duck typing system that allows us to create objects on the fly while keeping type safety. The following example shows how we can pass objects that don't explicitly implement an interface but contain all of the required members to a function:

```
function addPoints(p1: IPoint, p2: IPoint): IPoint {
    var x = p1.x + p2.x;
    var y = p1.y + p2.y;
    return { x: x, y: y }
}
//Valid
var newPoint = addPoints({ x: 3, y: 4 }, { x: 5, y: 1 });
//Error
var newPoint2 = addPoints({ x: 1 }, { x: 4, y: 3 });
```

Classes

In the next version of JavaScript, ECMAScript 6, a standard has been proposed for the definition of classes. TypeScript brings this concept to the current versions of JavaScript. Classes consist of a variety of different properties and members. These members can be either public or private and static or instance members.

Definitions

Creating classes in TypeScript is essentially the same as creating interfaces. Let's create a very simple Point class that keeps track of an x and a y position for us:

```
class Point {
    public x: number;
    public y: number;
    constructor(x: number, y = 0) {
        this.x = x;
        this.y = y;
    }
}
```

As you can see, defining a class is very simple. Use the keyword `class` and then provide a name for the new type. Then you create a constructor for the object with any parameters you wish to provide upon creation. Our `Point` class requires two values that represent a location on a plane.

> The constructor is completely optional. If a constructor implementation is not provided, the compiler will automatically generate one that takes no parameters and initializes any instance members.

We provided a default value for the property `y`. This default value tells the compiler to generate an extra JavaScript statement than if we had only given it a type. This also allows TypeScript to treat parameters with default values as optional parameters. If the parameter is not provided then the parameter's value is assigned to the default value you provide. This provides a simple method for ensuring that you are always operating on instantiated objects. The best part is that default values are available for all functions, not just constructors. Now let's examine the JavaScript output for the `Point` class:

```
var Point = (function () {
    function Point(x, y) {
        if (typeof y === "undefined") { y = 0; }
        this.x = x;
        this.y = y;
    }
    return Point;
})();
```

As you can see, a new object is created and assigned to an anonymous function that initializes the definition of the `Point` class. As we will see later, any public methods or static members will be added to the inner `Point` function's prototype. JavaScript closures are a very important concept in understanding TypeScript. Classes, modules, and enums in TypeScript all compile into JavaScript closures. Closures are actually a construct of the JavaScript language that provide a way of creating a private state for a specific segment of code. When a closure is created it contains two things: a function, and the state of the environment when the function was created. The function is returned to the caller of the closure and the state is used when the function is called.

> For more information about JavaScript closures and the module pattern visit http://www.adequatelygood.com/JavaScript-Module-Pattern-In-Depth.html.

The optional parameter was accounted for by checking its type and initializing it if a value is not available. You can also see that both x and y properties were added to the new instance and assigned to the values that were passed into the constructor.

Interfaces

Let's revisit our discussion of interfaces for a moment and look at how they interact with classes. In the next example, we will enforce the IPoint interface upon the Point class. Classes can optionally inherit type information from interfaces using the implements keyword. The class will then be required to implement all of the interface members; otherwise, compile errors will occur:

```
interface IPoint {
    x: number;
    y: number;
}
class Point implements IPoint {
    constructor(public x: number, public y = 0) {
    }
}
```

As we discussed earlier, interfaces are a purely compile time construct. The JavaScript that is output from this example is completely identical to the JavaScript we just saw. I snuck in a shorthand method of defining instance variables on classes too. Decorating the constructor's parameters with the public or private keywords tells TypeScript to treat these objects as part of the type and not just initialization parameters.

Classes are not limited to implementing a single interface. Providing a comma separated list of interfaces after the implements keyword allows your class to provide implementations of a variety of different contracts. Let's make our Point class more useful by implementing a second interface, as follows:

```
interface IPoint {
    x: number;
    y: number;
}
interface ICompare {
    Compare(p2: IPoint): number;
}
class Point implements IPoint, ICompare {
    public x: number;
    public y: number;
    constructor(x: number, y = 0) {
```

```
            this.x = x;
            this.y = y;
        }
    public Compare(p2: IPoint): number {
        var p1Val = this.x * this.x + this.y * this.y;
        var p2Val = p2.x * p2.x + p2.y * p2.y;
        var result = p1Val - p2Val;
        if (result == 0) {
            return 0;
        } else if (result > 0) {
            return 1;
        } else {
            return -1;
        }
    }
}
}
```

The ability to enforce multiple interfaces on our classes provides us with the ability to use our objects in several different contexts. Keeping our interfaces simple allows them to be more reusable across our applications. We could have easily placed the Compare method on the IPoint interface and achieved the same result. However, as we will see later with a few tweaks, any number of types could implement the ICompare interface, which have no need for the members x and y. In this case, the Compare method determines the distance each point is from the origin and returns a number representing which one is farthest away. If the object performing the comparison is farther away, a positive value is returned. If the point that has been passed as a parameter is farther away then a negative value is returned. If the two points are equivalent distances from the origin then a value of zero is returned.

Static and instance members

Both x and y are instance members of the class Point; this means that an object of the type Point must be instantiated for them to be referenced. When the constructor is called, values are assigned to properties of the object instance being created. These values can either be new objects created within the constructor function or references to objects passed in as the constructor parameters. This is a good thing for certain members, however, there are other class members that you may want access to even when an object has not been created. TypeScript provides this ability through static members. Static members are accessible at any time by referencing the named type. To declare a static member you simply decorate it with the static keyword:

```
class Point implements IPoint, ICompare {
    public x: number;
    public y: number;
    constructor(x: number, y = 0) {
```

```
        this.x = x;
        this.y = y;
    }
    public Compare(p2: IPoint): number {
        var p1Val = this.x * this.x + this.y * this.y;
        var p2Val = p2.x * p2.x + p2.y * p2.y;
        var result = p1Val - p2Val;
        if (result == 0) {
            return 0;
        } else if (result > 0) {
            return 1;
        } else {
            return -1;
        }
    }
    static Compare(p1: Point, p2: Point): number {
        return p1.Compare(p2);
    }
}
```

The preceding Compare method takes in two Point objects and compares their
distance from the origin to determine which is greater. The JavaScript output for
this class member is very different from that of the x and y properties being created
in the constructor. The following output shows that the Compare method is put
directly on the Point object being created:

```
var Point = (function () {
    function Point(x, y) {
        if (typeof y === "undefined") { y = 0; }
        this.x = x;
        this.y = y;
    }
    Point.prototype.Compare = function (p2) {
        var p1Val = this.x * this.x + this.y * this.y;
        var p2Val = p2.x * p2.x + p2.y * p2.y;
        var result = p1Val - p2Val;
        if (result == 0) {
            return 0;
        } else if (result > 0) {
            return 1;
        } else {
            return -1;
        }
    };
```

```
        Point.Compare = function (p1, p2) {
            return p1.Compare(p2);
        };
        return Point;
    })();
```

We still haven't discussed one of the most important parts of TypeScript classes, and that's instance member functions. These functions are only available to an instance of the object of the type and they have access to the `this` object that allows easy access to all of an object's members. In JavaScript, there are a couple of ways to create instance member functions. They can be added directly to the object using the `this` object during the object's creation, or they can be attached to the object's prototype. There are advantages and disadvantages to both, but it is generally better to put functions on the prototype rather than assign them to each new instance of the class. The instance of the function placed on the static prototype is then reused over and over rather than being recreated with each new instance of the type. This helps reduce memory consumption and will improve performance as your applications grow. TypeScript has adopted this method for attaching methods to instances of an object.

Let's create a new type that represents an object on a plane. It will have three properties: `Height`, `Width`, and `Location`. There will also be one instance member function that determines the size of the object on the plane. The `Location` member will be of type Point that we created just a little while ago:

```
interface IBounds {
    Location: IPoint;
    Height: number;
    Width: number;
    Size(): number;
}
class Bounds implements IBounds {
    public Location: IPoint = new Point(0, 0);
    public Height: number = 0;
    public Width: number = 0;
    public Size() {
        return this.Height * this.Width;
    }
}
```

As you can see, this class does not contain an explicit constructor; however, all of its properties are initialized and will be available for consumption when an instance of the type is created. As you can see from the resulting JavaScript, the `Size` method is placed on the `Bounds` object's static prototype member and a parameter-less constructor is created where all of the instance members are initialized:

```
var Bounds = (function () {
    function Bounds() {
        this.Location = new Point(0, 0);
        this.Height = 0;
        this.Width = 0;
    }
    Bounds.prototype.Size = function () {
        return this.Height * this.Width;
    };
    return Bounds;
})();
```

Properties

In ECMAScript 5, the concept of properties was introduced. This allows a developer to create getter and setter methods for a designated instance method that can be accessed like properties. If you have your TypeScript project set to compile ECMAScript 5, then you will be able to use the get and set keywords to define properties according to the ECMAScript 5 language specification. The ECMAScript version can be changed in the **General** settings of the TypeScript Build section of the project properties as shown in the following screenshot:

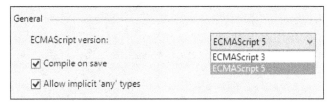

Let's modify our bounds class to treat both `Height` and `Width` as object properties rather than simple instance members and create both getter and setter methods for them both. The getters and setters will modify private instance members too, which will maintain the actual value. It is common practice in JavaScript to name private instance members with a leading underscore, so we will create _height and _width instance members for the `Bounds` class to access internally.

Since we now have a method block in which we can execute some code we should also provide some value checking to ensure correct program execution. The height and width of an object should never be less than zero so let's verify that the values being assigned to them fit this constraint; if not, we will set the value to zero manually:

```
interface IBounds {
    Location: IPoint;
    Height: number;
    Width: number;
    Size(): number;
}
class Bounds implements IBounds {
    public Location: IPoint = new Point(0, 0);
    private _height: number = 0;
    private _width: number = 0;
    public Size() {
        return this.Height * this.Width;
    }

    get Height(): number {
        return this._height;
    }
    set Height(value: number) {
        this._height = (value > 0) ? value : 0;
    }

    get Width(): number {
        return this._width;
    }
    set Width(value: number) {
        this._width = (value > 0) ? value : 0;
    }
}
```

As you can see, we now have method blocks wrapping the access of the Height and Width properties. The properties are still accessed as if they were instance variables as you can see from the Size method, however, our function blocks are executed when we access them. The resulting JavaScript calls the Object.defineProperty method, outlined in the ECMAScript 5 standard, when the type is created.

While the ECMAScript 5 standard has been widely adopted by most browsers, it is important to note that there are some lapses in feature support in certain browsers. The table found at the following link outlines the current support for the ECMAScript 5 standard: `http://kangax.github.io/compat-table/es5/`.

This places a new object on the prototype that is accessible on all instances of that type. The following JavaScript is what is generated by defining getters and setters in TypeScript:

```
var Bounds = (function () {
    function Bounds() {
        this.Location = new Point(0, 0);
        this._height = 0;
        this._width = 0;
    }
    Bounds.prototype.Size = function () {
        return this.Height * this.Width;
    };

    Object.defineProperty(Bounds.prototype, "Height", {
        get: function () {
            return this._height;
        },
        set: function (value) {
            this._height = (value > 0) ? value : 0;
        },
        enumerable: true,
        configurable: true
    });

    Object.defineProperty(Bounds.prototype, "Width", {
        get: function () {
            return this._width;
        },
        set: function (value) {
            this._width = (value > 0) ? value : 0;
        },
        enumerable: true,
        configurable: true
    });
    return Bounds;
})();
```

There are a few other notables from this output to consider. We created new private variables to store the values being surfaced by our property declarations. These private variables are being added to each instance of the object in the constructor. This seems a little strange since we know that closures can store a private state for each instance of the class. The reason that private variables need to be added to each instance is because the functions and properties are attached to the prototype on the class. The prototype does not retain the state of the closure and relies on the actual object instance to access its members.

The IBounds interface is still upheld after converting to properties as well. The resulting type information from creating an instance of the class just has to match that of the interface for compilation. There is no distinction made between whether it is an instance member or a property declaration because they are both accessed in the same manner.

We have covered quite a bit here in a very short period of time. Classes are one of the most important concepts introduced by TypeScript that help turn JavaScript into an enterprise-level development platform. We still have a number of concepts to cover, including enums.

Enums

Enums are a useful entity intended for holding a specific value that is referenced using a friendly name to keep code readable. An enum value is nothing more than an integer that is associated with a named constant. Enums are very simple to declare, however, it is what they generate in JavaScript that makes them interesting. First, let's look at an enum declaration and then we will go over the result:

```
enum ShapeType {
    Rectangle,
    Circle,
    Line,
    Freehand
}
```

The declaration of an enum type takes the type name for referencing the enum and then the body is just a list of possible values separated by commas. There's nothing particularly special about this from a TypeScript perspective. You can access the enum values like you were accessing a class's static members: ShapeType.Rectangle. As I said earlier though, the real magic behind enums in TypeScript is how they are generated in JavaScript, so let's take a look at the output of our enum:

```
var ShapeType;
(function (ShapeType) {
```

```
    ShapeType[ShapeType["Rectangle"] = 0] = "Rectangle";
    ShapeType[ShapeType["Circle"] = 1] = "Circle";
    ShapeType[ShapeType["Line"] = 2] = "Line";
    ShapeType[ShapeType["Freehand"] = 3] = "Freehand";
})(ShapeType || (ShapeType = {}));
```

There is quite a bit of JavaScript here to represent something as simple as number mapping. However, if you look at it more deeply you will see that TypeScript is creating a two-way mapping between the named constant and the number it is mapped to. This creates a number of interesting ways in which you can access the values of an enum. Take a look at the following code snippet and consider what the output might be:

```
    alert(ShapeType[ShapeType.Rectangle]);
```

ShapeType has been created inside of an anonymous function that returns an object that has been given two properties for each member of the enum. Taking advantage of JavaScript's dynamic typing system, TypeScript adds a property with the string value of the member name and maps it to an integer value. That integer value is then simultaneously added as a property of the ShapeType object and is mapped to the string value of the named member. So if you thought that the value returned previously was the string representation of the named member, then you were correct!

Now that we are familiar with how an enum works, let's look some more at the individual members of an enum. We know that enums represent two-way mapping between a number and a string, but where does that number come from? In the ShapeType example, we just saw each member was just given a name, the number was generated by the compiler. This works well and creates a sequential set of numbers for us to access, but a little more control over these values would be nice. TypeScript has therefore provided two types of enum members that can be created: constant members, and computed members. What we looked at earlier were all constant members with auto-generated constant values. These numbers are sequential starting from zero unless a constant value is provided to a member. Then, all of the subsequent members of the enum will be in sequence with the number given.

Computed members are still named constants but the integer value they are mapped to is provided by an expression. This can be either an inline expression or a function call to another segment of code. The only stipulation on the expression that you provide is that it returns a number. As you can see in the following code segment, we have modified our previous enum, ShapeType, to generate some specific indexes as well as create a computed member:

```
function GetEnumValue(): number {
    return Date.now();
}
enum ShapeType {
    Rectangle = 3,
    Circle,
    Line,
    Freehand,
    Random = GetEnumValue()
}
```

As you can see, we have created a function that returns an integer representing the current time using the global Date object available in JavaScript. We also set the first constant member to an integer value of our choosing. When the compiler parses this, all of the members in the enum will grow sequentially from this value. Let's take a look at the resulting JavaScript now and see how a computed member will look at runtime:

```
function GetEnumValue() {
    return Date.now();
}
var ShapeType;
(function (ShapeType) {
    ShapeType[ShapeType["Rectangle"] = 3] = "Rectangle";
    ShapeType[ShapeType["Circle"] = 4] = "Circle";
    ShapeType[ShapeType["Line"] = 5] = "Line";
    ShapeType[ShapeType["Freehand"] = 6] = "Freehand";
    ShapeType[ShapeType["Random"] = GetEnumValue()] = "Random";
})(ShapeType || (ShapeType = {}));
```

As you can see, the expression provided to the computed member is built directly into the enum declaration generated. This expression will be evaluated at runtime but only when ShapeType is initialized. Once the expression has been run, the result will remain a member of the ShapeType object. Therefore, in the preceding example ShapeType.Random is equivalent to ShapeType.Random as long as the ShapeType enum stays in memory. You may be wondering right now what the usefulness is of being able to change the constant members' numeric sequence.

The one piece of information we haven't covered on enums so far is that their definitions can be merged. If two enum declarations are placed in different segments of code with the same type name they will contribute to the same object. You can see this in the last line of the enum declaration in the resulting JavaScript. If the object exists then each new property is added to the existing object; otherwise, a new object is created and the properties are applied.

Modules

The module pattern has become increasingly popular in JavaScript development. It provides an easy way to encapsulate private members, something that isn't inherently available in JavaScript, and keep objects off the global namespace. In TypeScript there are two types of modules: **internal modules** and **external modules**. We will discuss them both in detail, but for now let's just talk about internal modules.

Internal modules

Internal modules represent a namespace that classes, interfaces, enums, variables, code segments, and other namespaces can exist inside of. They are created inside of a closure just like classes are. However, modules don't return a function that gets assigned to a global variable. Modules execute the closure with a global variable as a parameter. Exported properties are then attached to this global variable. A module can contain any number of declarations of any type of object including other modules. Each of the declarations inside of a module can be either kept isolated or they can be exported. Exported objects will be added to the module's instance. In the following code segment, you can see an internal module definition:

```
module Shapes {
    var origin: IPoint = new Point(0, 0);
    export interface IShape {
        Type: ShapeType;
        Bounds: IBounds;
    }
    export class Shape implements IShape {
        public Type: ShapeType = ShapeType.Rectangle;
        public Bounds: IBounds = new Bounds();
    }
}
```

In this example, we see a mix of both private members and public members that exist on the Shapes module. The origin variable is a private instance of the Point class we created earlier. Any expression inside the Shapes module has access to the origin variable but since it is not decorated with the export keyword, it is limited to within the module. We have defined an interface for an object type that will represent a shape of some sort. Then we also have a new class that implements the shape interface and is ready to be drawn on a surface. This Shape object needs to be accessible outside the Shapes namespace so we must export it. Our ShapeType enum probably belongs within the Shapes namespace so let's move its declaration to within the module definition as well:

```
module Shapes {
    var origin: IPoint = new Point(0, 0);
    export enum ShapeType {
        Rectangle = 3,
        Circle,
        Line,
        Freehand,
    }
    export interface IShape {
        Type: ShapeType;
        Bounds: IBounds;
    }
    export class Shape {
        public Type: ShapeType = ShapeType.Rectangle;
        public Bounds: IBounds = new Bounds();
    }
}
```

We now have an internal module that has two accessible named types, the ShapeType enum and Shape class, and one inaccessible variable, the origin variable, which is part of the isolated state of the module. While we may not necessarily need access to the ShapeType enum it still must be exported for our code to compile. Any named types that are used in the definition of another member must be made as accessible as that member. If this requirement is not met compilation will fail. Accessing these types is done by providing the module name and then the type you wish to access. In the following example, you can see we create a new Shape object and set its type:

```
var shape = new Shapes.Shape();
shape.Type = Shapes.ShapeType.Circle;
```

The JavaScript generated for this module looks very similar to the code generated for enum types. All of the members of the module are wrapped in a closure that runs when the module is loaded. Each of the exported types is placed on the instance variable that is passed to the closure that it is available to anyone accessing the module. Modules also share the same ability to be merged that enums do. This means that you can separate your code into multiple files and have them merged into one object during runtime. The downside to this implementation of modules is that it takes away the ability to create interfaces for your modules. However, the ability to organize your code in whichever manner you choose is far more valuable than any functionality interfaces would bring to modules. Here, you can see the resulting JavaScript that TypeScript creates to define its modules:

```
var Shapes;
(function (Shapes) {
    var origin = new Point(0, 0);
    (function (ShapeType) {
        ShapeType[ShapeType["Rectangle"] = 3] = "Rectangle";
        ShapeType[ShapeType["Circle"] = 4] = "Circle";
        ShapeType[ShapeType["Line"] = 5] = "Line";
        ShapeType[ShapeType["Freehand"] = 6] = "Freehand";
    })(Shapes.ShapeType || (Shapes.ShapeType = {}));
    var ShapeType = Shapes.ShapeType;
    var Shape = (function () {
        function Shape() {
            this.Type = 3 /* Rectangle */;
            this.Bounds = new Bounds();
            this.Bounds.Location = origin;
        }
        return Shape;
    })();
    Shapes.Shape = Shape;
})(Shapes || (Shapes = {}));
```

So far we've only seen a small example of a module, but imagine building a large-scale application with a large amount of object types. You will want to create namespaces to organize your code and create a layer of separation between segments of code that are unrelated. There are two ways to provide module namespaces in TypeScript. We can nest the modules inside of each other or we can define them as part of the module declaration.

Let's take a look at some of the different ways to define namespaces and create module definitions.

```
module Animals {
    export module Reptiles {
        export var snake = "snake";
    }
}
module Animals.Mammals {
    export var monkey = "monkey";
}
```

In this example, we create a declaration for the `Animals` module and then nest another module declaration inside of it that gets exported. There is also a module declaration that is given a multi-part type name separated by the . character. Both of the module declarations shown are valid. The JavaScript output from both declarations is exactly the same so which style you choose is really a matter of preference. The compiler will treat them as equivalents as will the development environment. As you can see in the following screenshot, accessing both the `Reptiles` and `Mammals` namespaces is identical:

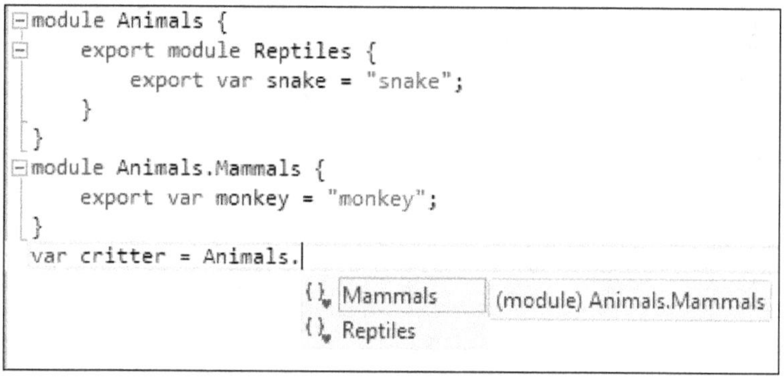

The resulting JavaScript from each of these module definitions is identical in structure. However, if you intend on declaring multiple nested modules inside of a single TypeScript file, it is best to use the expanded nesting declaration rather than the shortcut. The compiler will not attempt to optimize and merge the module definitions when it creates the JavaScript output. As you can see in the following JavaScript code, you will unnecessarily have multiple closures adding objects to the type object. This is inevitable if you intend on separating your namespaces by file.

```
var Animals;
(function (Animals) {
```

```
    (function (Reptiles) {
        Reptiles.snake = "snake";
    })(Animals.Reptiles || (Animals.Reptiles = {}));
    var Reptiles = Animals.Reptiles;
})(Animals || (Animals = {}));
var Animals;
(function (Animals) {
    (function (Mammals) {
        Mammals.monkey = "monkey";
    })(Animals.Mammals || (Animals.Mammals = {}));
    var Mammals = Animals.Mammals;
})(Animals || (Animals = {}));
```

There are probably some common object types or utility methods that you would prefer to have quick access to inside of another module. As we continue to separate our types appropriately let's create a new module for drawing-related functionality. This module will contain both the `Point` class and the `Bounds` class that we created earlier. Both of these classes will be exported because other modules will need to be able to reference them. While it is nice to have the code separated into isolated segments that can be easily managed, I now have to provide a fully qualified name every time I wish to use a type from another module. Thankfully, TypeScript has provided a keyword opposite to the export keyword that allows us to create an alias to members of another module. The `import` keyword creates a new local reference to exported types from other modules. In the following code segment, we will create an alias for the `Bounds` class inside the `Shapes` module. This will prevent us from having to change the definition of our `Shape` class to contain the full namespace of the `Bounds` type.

```
module Shapes {
    import Bounds = Drawing.Bounds;
    export enum ShapeType {
        Rectangle = 3,
        Circle,
        Line,
        Freehand,
    }
    export interface IShape {
        Type: ShapeType;
        Bounds: Drawing.IBounds;
    }
    export class Shape {
        public Type: ShapeType = ShapeType.Rectangle;
        public Bounds: Drawing.IBounds = new Bounds();
    }
}
```

As you can see, the alias can be used as both a type annotation and as its object type. The resulting JavaScript just replaces the import keyword with `var` and lets the runtime engine create the reference to the exported member. However, doing this directly in TypeScript will generate a compile error. The `import` keyword informs the compiler not to inspect just the object being aliased but its type information as well so that it can be used in type declarations.

> The `export` and `import` keywords can be used in conjunction to create externally accessible aliases.

Generic objects

If your goal when adopting TypeScript is to create an API for client consumption, then generics are the language construct you should become the most familiar with. They allow consumers of frameworks and APIs to agree on a specific contract to accomplish a designated goal without having to know specific object types. Generics define the third and final category of objects in TypeScript, type parameters. As we saw earlier in this chapter when we discussed arrays, type parameters are defined inside of < and > characters. They can be used on interfaces or class definitions to create functionality for a broad set of object types that may or may not be known at the time of development. Let's say we wanted to create a generic task processor. We will assume the simplest possible implementation, which is just a sequential process that passes a list of generic tasks to a function to have them run:

```
interface ITask {
    Id: number;
    Execute(): boolean;
    Error: string;
}
function ProcessTasks<T extends ITask>(tasks: T[]): T {
    for (var i = 0; i < tasks.length; i++) {
        if (tasks[i].Execute() == false) {
            return tasks[i];
        }
    }
    return null;
}
```

In this example, we have defined an interface that the task processor will rely on to execute a set of tasks sequentially. The function declaration for `ProcessTasks` now contains a type parameter, `T`, which must adhere to the `ITask` interface. This type parameter is used as a constraint for the objects that can be passed in as part of the tasks array, and will be the return type of the function. The tasks array is looped through one by one and the `Execute` method is called. If the `Execute` method returns a false value then the processing is stopped and the task is returned. Generics are built completely on type annotations, so they have no effect on the generated JavaScript. However, if the type constraints are not met, a compile error will be generated.

Interfaces and classes are capable of creating even more complex structures built around a very loose type definition. A type parameter provided to an interface or class can be used to provide type information for any member or function inside of the declaration body. In the next example, our `ProcessTasks` function has been moved into a class that will operate as the processor. A generic interface is created that will allow us to create any number of task processors with different implementations of the `ProcessTasks` function. Then, we see a class declaration that provides its own set of type parameters and implements the `ITaskProcessor` interface:

```
interface ITask {
    Id: number;
    Execute(): boolean;
    Error: string;
}
interface ITaskProcessor<T extends ITask> {
    ProcessTasks(tasks: Array<T>): T;
    CurrentTask: T;
}
class TaskProcessor<T extends ITask> implements ITaskProcessor<T> {
    public CurrentTask: T = null;
    constructor() {
    }
    public ProcessTasks(tasks: T[]): T {
        for (var i = 0; i < tasks.length; i++) {
            this.CurrentTask = tasks[i];
            if (this.CurrentTask.Execute() == false) {
                return tasks[i];
            }
        }
        this.CurrentTask = null;
        return null;
    }
}
```

Generic functions and types are not limited to a single unknown type. Type parameters can be lists of type information that can be used anywhere within the declaration block that the list is associated with. Creating a list of type parameters is the same as passing a single type parameter, only each type is separated by a comma. Furthermore, each generic type created in a parameter list can be used as a base type for other type parameters inside of the type's definition. The next example shows both of these concepts:

```
interface IExample<T, U extends HTMLElement> {
    Operate<V extends U>(): T;
}
```

As you can see, there is a comma-separated list of generic types and any constraints they might have instead of the single generic type. The `Operate` function then requires a type that inherits from the `U` type that was provided in the initial type parameter list.

Summary

This chapter has thoroughly discussed the different language constructs in TypeScript. We covered all three of the type categories: primitive types, object types, and type parameters. Primitive types are ones that have been built into the language such as Number, Boolean, and String. Object types range from classes to modules and allow us to construct organized components in our applications. Type parameters allow us to create generic functions and objects that can be used to operate on a variety of types. TypeScript relies heavily on JavaScript's closures when it is generating the different object types. Next, we are going to be looking at the TypeScript compiler and its various options.

The TypeScript Compiler

3

In this chapter, the TypeScript compiler will be analyzed. The different parameters that the compiler understands will be broken down and explained, as well as how they affect the ECMAScript that gets generated. We will discuss how to control where your code gets generated to, as well as the different files that can accompany our generated ECMAScript. There are also a few other options available on the compiler that make building and deploying large scale applications easier.

The topics that will be covered in the chapter are as follows:

- ECMAScript generation
- Output control
- Advanced compiler options

Generation of ECMAScript

As with most programming languages, ECMAScript has evolved over time. It was initially developed in the mid-nineties for use in client-side scripting. The current standard is ECMAScript 5; however, Version 6 is currently being worked on. The TypeScript compiler provides a list of options to change the way your code is generated. In this section, we will look at these options and compare the results.

ECMAScript version

Writing JavaScript code means your code must be portable across multiple types of client devices and browsers. You may be forced to not only support the latest version of a browser but potentially any of its previous versions. For this reason, the compiler supports compiling your TypeScript code into different versions of ECMAScript. ECMAScript 3 was a widely adopted and heavily used standard and has survived in many legacy browsers. ECMAScript 4 was abandoned when the group responsible for creating the standard could not agree on the language features. ECMAScript 5 is the current standard and has been adopted by most current browsers. It was published in 2009, nearly a decade after Version 3 was initially published. In *Chapter 2, TypeScript Basics*, we saw that you could easily switch between versions of ECMAScript in Visual Studio. Let's take a look at what is actually going on behind the scenes when we change this option. In the following screenshot, you can see that we call the compiler the same way we did in *Chapter 1, Getting Started with TypeScript*, only this time we have provided an additional parameter:

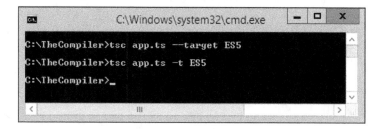

As you can see, there are two ways of passing the ECMAScript target version to the compiler: the verbose method -target and the shorthand method -t.

> If a target version is not supplied, the compiler will default to ECMAScript 3. So, unless you are explicitly using language constructs only defined in ECMAScript 5, this parameter does not need to be provided.

ECMAScript 5 was originally slated to be a minor update, ECMAScript 3.1, and provide only a limited set of new features in an attempt to maintain backwards compatibility. Strict mode was introduced, which provides a set of different semantic rules to the language. There are three primary changes that strict mode makes to normal ECMAScript semantics:

- Certain silent errors are now thrown
- Enforces rules that allow the language engine to provide more optimizations
- Ensures that certain keywords can't be used to allow future versions of ECMAScript to have them available for the language specification

While the option to use strict mode is still available in TypeScript by placing `use strict` at the top of your TypeScript file, its value is less significant. The TypeScript compiler accounts for most of the rules enforced on JavaScript code that is run in strict mode. For instance, if you attempt to assign a value to a variable that does not exist or is not defined, a compile error will be generated. When running your JavaScript out of strict mode this will create a new variable and put it in the global scope. If this is done in JavaScript running in strict mode, a reference error will be generated. The `with` keyword creates a syntax error in strict JavaScript because optimizations are not able to be made on code blocks within the declaration block. TypeScript will generate a syntax error any time you attempt to use a `with` block. The TypeScript compiler will even format your existing JavaScript to a more restricted set of standards, for instance, if you write the following lines of code:

```
function sayHello() {
    alert("Hello There")
}
SayHello()
```

In most cases this is legal JavaScript; however, under certain circumstances semicolons are required to keep the code meaningful. When the compiler finishes generating this code it has recognized the missing semicolons and added them to the resulting JavaScript:

```
function sayHello() {
    alert("Hello There");
}
SayHello();
```

As we discussed in the previous chapter, TypeScript adds a large number of language constructs that the current version of ECMAScript is lacking. However, the language will continue to evolve and new constructs will be added to the specification. Strict mode helps prevent developers from creating code that uses potential keywords for future versions. The keywords prevented in strict mode are: `implements`, `interface`, `let`, `package`, `private`, `protected`, `public`, `static`, and `yield`. As you can see, there is a fair amount of overlap between what TypeScript defines and what has been set aside by the language committee for future use. We have already discussed the TypeScript implementations of `implements`, `interface`, `private`, `public`, and `static`. The remaining names, restricted by strict mode, are currently keywords in TypeScript; however, any attempt to use them will result in a compile error.

There is really only one key construct that you should avoid if you want your code to be compatible with both ECMAScript 3 and 5, and that is getters and setters. Getters and setters are used to define properties for JavaScript objects. They are a special type of language construct that allows them to be accessed like variables but internally they are implemented as functions. Browser compatibility for getters and setters can be found in the table referenced in *Chapter 2, TypeScript Basics*. The following code snippet shows how these properties are created:

```
interface IBook {
    title: string;
}
class Book implements IBook {
    private _title: string = "";
    constructor() {
    }
    get title(): string {
        return this._title;
    }
    set title(value: string) {
        if (value && value.length > 0) {
            this._title = value;
        } else {
            throw ("Invalid Book Title!");
        }
    }
}
```

We are now able to wrap the process of assigning or retrieving the title of the book in a function declaration. In this case, a book must have a title, so attempting to set it to null or an empty string results in an exception being generated. If you attempt to run this code through the compiler and do not set the target version to ES5, you will receive an error that looks similar to the following screenshot:

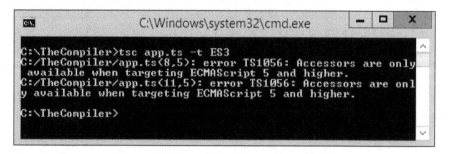

Code manipulation

There are a couple of other options available for the compiler that will determine what the resulting JavaScript code will look like. Like JavaScript, TypeScript allows comments to be placed within the code. They are defined exactly the same way JavaScript comments are and they have no effect on runtime execution. Comments are used to explain what a segment of code, is designed to do, so that when another developer has to look at the code they will know what is going on. This can be very helpful when stepping through our code during development. However, when the code is deployed to a client, these comments are unnecessary and add to the size of our JavaScript files. Using the -removeComments parameter, we can ensure that all of this unneeded data is removed before deployment. Consider the following TypeScript code:

```
//Retrieve a new random integer value
function getRandom(): number {
    return Math.floor(Math.random() * Date.now());
}
```

The preceding code can be compiled using the command shown in the following screenshot:

This results in the following JavaScript output:

```
function getRandom() {
    return Math.floor(Math.random() * Date.now());
}
```

On a small scale, this doesn't represent a huge gain; however, when you scale the application up to have hundreds of thousands of lines of code, this could represent a significant amount of data. It is common practice in JavaScript development to minify your .js files when you push them into production. This helps reduce the overall file size and has no effect on runtime speed. Unfortunately, the TypeScript compiler does not have an option for this upon the release of Version 1.0. Hopefully, it will be added in future versions but there are other tools available to minify JavaScript in the meantime. RequireJS is a library that we will talk about later on, and it provides options to minify JavaScript code.

The final ECMAScript output-related parameter available for the TypeScript compiler is the module parameter. This parameter tells the compiler how to generate code for external modules. There are two very common patterns used for the implementation of external modules: CommonJS (used in Node.js) and AMD (provided by RequireJS). Each one provides its own syntax and keywords to help define external modules. TypeScript uses the same syntax to represent both and provides the compiler option to define the result. The following code segment defines an external module in TypeScript:

```
export module CompilerExample {
    var verify = "Success!";
    export function test() {
        alert(verify);
    }
}
```

As you can see, our top level module is now decorated with the export keyword. This defines the external module in TypeScript but external modules aren't a construct in JavaScript so third-party libraries are used. If we compile this code using the module parameter and give it a value of amd, then the compiler will generate the modules consumable using RequireJS:

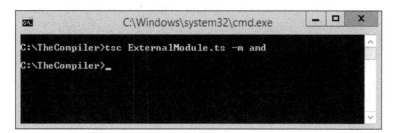

Then our generated JavaScript will be the following:

```
define(["require", "exports"], function(require, exports) {
    (function (CompilerExample) {
        var verify = "Success!";
        function test() {
            alert(verify);
        }
        CompilerExample.test = test;
    })(exports.CompilerExample || (exports.CompilerExample = {}));
    var CompilerExample = exports.CompilerExample;
});
```

We will discuss exactly what this code is doing later in our discussion of external modules but as you can see, a closure is generated and two objects are passed in for use in generation of the module. The CommonJS module pattern looks very different from this though. Running the same command only providing `commonjs` for the module parameters value will generate the following output:

```
(function (CompilerExample) {
    var verify = "Success!";
    function test() {
        alert(verify);
    }
    CompilerExample.test = test;
}) (exports.CompilerExample || (exports.CompilerExample = {}));
var CompilerExample = exports.CompilerExample;
```

As you can see, the resulting JavaScript is very different; however, nothing about our TypeScript changed.

Controlling compiler output

The TypeScript compiler has a very robust set of features when it comes to controlling the final results of the compiler. The compiler is built in a scalable manner that allows us to compile multiple source files at once as well as controlling their output directory or path. We will also discuss creating source maps that help us when debugging our applications.

JavaScript output

Up until this point, we have only been working with compiling single TypeScript files at a time. As applications grow in size though, it is very important to separate our code into maintainable segments. When writing code for a C# application, it is common to separate code files by class. JavaScript conventions vary in how code is segmented. If following the module pattern, it is common to place an entire module in a single file; otherwise, code is usually segmented into related blocks as the application requires them. Passing multiple file names separated by spaces will tell the compiler to parse each file and generate a JavaScript file for each. The following screenshot shows how this is done:

As you can see, we now have two TypeScript files and each is being passed to the compiler as a parameter. The result of running this command will be two JavaScript files, one for each corresponding TypeScript file. There is no limit to the number of files that can be provided; however, at some point the command line will reach its buffer limit. We will see in a little while how to make this easier through the use of a parameter file.

The TypeScript compiler provides two main options for controlling where the JavaScript that will be used at runtime is output to. The first option requires a folder location to output all of the generated JavaScript files separately. As you can see in the following screenshot, we use the --outDir parameter to provide our location:

The other option allows us to compile our TypeScript down into a single JavaScript file. This allows us to make a single HTTP GET request for our application rather than having to make multiple ones. This can be a very complex task to accomplish when an application grows in scale and each piece of code must be loaded in a certain order to ensure proper execution. The TypeScript compiler has a few different ways of ensuring that code generated in a single file is created in such a manner that all objects exist before they are needed. The simplest manner in which to ensure this is to manually provide the files in the order that they should be compiled. Let's look at our two TypeScript files and how they interact:

```
function sayHello() {
    alert("Hello There");
}
function getRandom(): number {
    return Math.floor(Math.random() * Date.now());
}
```

The preceding section of code represents a file called `utilities.ts` and is a collection of functions that can be used to do a variety of different things. The next segment of code is `app.ts` and it references both of these functions and relies on them to be available at runtime.

```
SayHello();
alert(GetRandom());
```

If we were to generate these into separate JavaScript files then we would have to place multiple script tags in our HTML pages. The script tags would have to be provided in a specific order, otherwise a reference error would occur and the application would stop working. We already have to provide multiple TypeScript files to the compiler, so why not just generate a single JavaScript file and avoid having to deal with this? The following screenshot shows how to specify a single file location for all of our generated JavaScript:

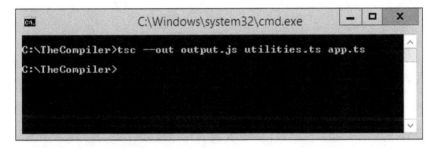

This will result in the concatenation of the two resulting JavaScript files that are generated by the compiler. This means that our TypeScript files must still be provided in the proper order, otherwise a reference error will occur. Thankfully, TypeScript provides a way to help control this problem using a particular syntax to determine a reference graph. The next code segment shows how to provide a specific reference to another TypeScript file to ensure the proper order is upheld by the compiler:

```
/// <reference path="utilities.ts" />
sayHello();
alert(getRandom());
```

These references should be made at the very top of your TypeScript files. If they are not, then the order your files are concatenated together in will be wrong. The compiler examines the beginning of each file and parses certain constructs to determine how the resulting JavaScript should be generated. Once the first block of execution code is reached, the compiler will stop looking for these syntax constructs. By providing this reference, we are now able to pass our TypeScript files to the compiler in any order that we want.

Run the command shown in the following screenshot:

The resulting JavaScript file will look like the following:

```
function sayHello() {
    alert("Hello There");
}
function getRandom() {
    return Math.floor(Math.random() * Date.now());
}
/// <reference path="utilities.ts" />
sayHello();
alert(getRandom());
```

As you can see, our final result is placed into a single `output.js` file and is in the proper order to ensure no reference errors are thrown. It is possible for two files to reference each other, however this is not recommended. If only one of the files references objects instantiated by the other file, the compiler will be able to order the JavaScript properly. Otherwise, it will be unable to guarantee that all of the referenced objects are available at runtime. This will not result in a compilation error, so be wary of creating such a situation.

Source maps

Next, we will look at source maps and how they allow us to step through our TypeScript code rather than just the generated JavaScript. Source maps are a useful tool created to help debug code that has already been combined and minified. TypeScript and Visual Studio take advantage of this by providing source maps that direct back to the original TypeScript files. The `--sourcemap` parameter tells the compiler to generate a map file for each JavaScript file generated. This map file is then used to help map each line segment of minified or combined code back to a non-minified file that is easier to debug. The map file generated by the TypeScript compiler will point the mappings to the original TypeScript files associated with the code being run.

The following screenshot shows how to generate source maps during compilation:

Now, both of our TypeScript files are combined into a single JavaScript file but if we want to debug them individually, we can. When the sourcemap parameter is provided, it tells the compiler to inject a new line into each generated JavaScript file directing the debugger to the source map that has been generated:

```
//# sourceMappingURL=output.js.map
```

In our case, the resulting map file is called output.js.map and is located in the same directory as output.js. The contents of this map file are as follows:

```
{
    "version":3,
    "file":"output.js",
    "sourceRoot":"",
    "sources":["utilities.ts","app.ts"],
    "names":["SayHello","GetRandom"],
    "mappings":"AACA,+BAD+B;AAC/B,SAAS,QAAQ;IACbA,KAAKA,CAACA,aAAaA,CA
ACA;AACxBA,CAACA;;AAED,KAAK,CAAC,SAAS,CAAC,CAAC,CAAC;ACL1B,qCAAqC;AACr
C,QAAQ,CAAC,CAAC;AACV,SAAS,SAAS;IACdC,OAAOA,IAAIA,CAACA,KAAKA,CAACA,IA
AIA,CAACA,MAAMA,CAACA,CAACA,GAAGA,IAAIA,CAACA,GAAGA,CAACA,CAACA,CAACA;
AACjDA,CAACA;AAED,mBAAmB;AACnB,oBAAoB;AACpB,GAAG;AACH,+BAA+B;AAC/B,kCA
AkC;AAC1C,qBAAqB;AACrB,OAAO;AACP,2BAA2B;AAC3B,6BAA6B;AAC7B,OAAO;AACP,g
CAAgC;AAChC,0CAA0C;AAC1C,kCAAkC;AAC1C,kBAAkB;AAC1B,4CAA4C;AAC5C,WAAW;A
ACX,OAAO;AACP,GAAG;AAAEH,qCAAqC"
}
```

As you can see, this is a very simple JSON object that contains the information necessary to map the JavaScript code that has been generated back to the TypeScript files that it originated from. The "sources" property contains the array of TypeScript files that we build. The "names" property represents named types that exist within the code, and "sourceRoot" is the location where the source files are located. If you have opted to specify an output file for your combined JavaScript that is in a different directory than your TypeScript files, it is important to specify the --sourceRoot if you intend to use the source map. The sourceRoot parameter should be a value that is relative to the location of your map file.

The following screenshot shows you how to configure your Visual Studio project to combine its JavaScript into a single file, generate a source map, and point that source map back to the original TypeScript files:

As you can see, we combine our TypeScript into a single JavaScript file in a subdirectory of the project. The **Generate source maps** checkbox has been selected so that `sourceMappingURL` is added to the resulting JavaScript. The **Specify root directory of TypeScript files** option has been selected and a relative path has been provided for the debugger to interpret. The **Specify root directory of source maps** option changes the location provided to the `sourceMappingURL` value. The TypeScript root directory and source map root directory options correspond to the `--sourceRoot` and `--mapRoot` respectively.

Advanced options

With everything we've seen so far, we can build and deploy large applications. Now, we are going to take a look at the few remaining options that we haven't covered yet. Some are just informative, while others can help you and your team write better TypeScript code. As with most command line utilities, the TypeScript compiler comes with a help parameter that will output all of the compiler's options. To view all of these options, use the `-h` or `--help` parameters or simply run the compiler with no parameters at all. There is also a version parameter that outputs the current version of the TypeScript compiler that is installed. This is viewed using either the `-v` or `--version` parameters. As you can see from the following screenshot, this book was written immediately following the initial release of TypeScript as a completed language.

Since the language is open source, expect improvements to be made and new versions to be available.

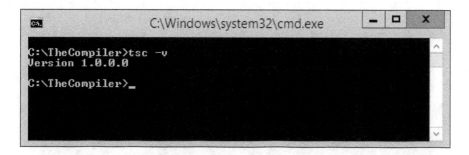

Now that we've covered the options that we'll use very infrequently, let's get back to improving how we develop for the Web. If you are writing a web application, it is possible you could have users all around the world. This means your applications could and probably should support multiple languages. To ensure that each localized character is displayed properly, you may have to specify a code page.

 A code page is a number that is used to represent character encoding. For instance, UTF-8 is 65001 while ASCII is 20127.

The TypeScript compiler provides the `--codepage` parameter to allow you to specify the character set that the resulting JavaScript file will contain. By default, the TypeScript compiler will use 65001 when this parameter is not provided. Visual Studio does not allow this option to be specified and UTF-8 should be used in most scenarios.

We talked earlier about JavaScript's strict mode and how it forced certain constructs upon the language that help improve the code we develop. TypeScript has its own version of strict mode that forces us to use types everywhere. If a type is not explicitly provided and the compiler is not able to infer the object's type information, we can use the compiler to warn us. To enforce this constraint, simply provide the `--noImplicitAny` parameter when compiling your TypeScript files. In the following code segment, you can see that we create a situation where the type variable `a` is not known. We do not provide it with initial type information and we assign it to multiple object types during execution.

```
function implicitType() {
    var a;
    a = 2;
    a = "bob";
    alert(a);
}
```

The final runtime value of a will be `"bob"`; however, this breaks the type safety that TypeScript aims to provide. In the following screenshot, you can see how to enforce types within your code and the result of attempting to compile the preceding code:

```
C:\Windows\system32\cmd.exe                              -  □  X

C:\TheCompiler>tsc --noImplicitAny app.ts
C:/TheCompiler/app.ts(26,9): error TS7006: Parameter 'a' of
'implicitType' implicitly has an 'any' type.

C:\TheCompiler>_
```

Enforcing types upon our code will not only help us to ensure we write solid code, but it will help anyone attempting to consume it on an API level or understand the intent of the code. Strongly typing our objects helps others know what they are working with. However, you don't want to have to provide all of your TypeScript source files to anyone consuming your code as an API. For this reason, TypeScript has created another language construct that will provide type information to consumers without providing any implementation details. This type information is placed into a declaration file, which can then be distributed along with the combined and minified JavaScript file that can be used at runtime. In the next segment of code, there is a module that is reusable and can be deployed for any JavaScript code to call:

```typescript
module MyNamespace {
    export interface IClass {
        Id: string;
        DoSomething();
    }
    export class MyClass implements IClass {
        constructor(public Id: string = Date.now().toString()) {
        }
        public DoSomething() {
            alert(this.Id);
        }
    }
}
```

This module can be consumed by other TypeScript files that are aware where the source file is. However, someone consuming only a JavaScript file will be unable to interact with our objects in a strongly typed fashion. If we provide the declaration file to our consumers though, they can use our objects as if they existed inside of their own code base. To generate the declaration file for a TypeScript file, run the command shown in the following screenshot:

During the compilation process, the type information for our module will be extracted into a new file that will be output alongside the resulting JavaScript file. It will have the format <filename>.d.ts and will be treated by any TypeScript compiler as a collection of type definitions. Attempting to place execution code in a declaration file will result in an error. The file generated from our module is as follows:

```
declare module MyNamespace {
    interface IClass {
        Id: string;
        DoSomething(): any;
    }
    class MyClass implements IClass {
        public Id: string;
        constructor(Id?: string);
        public DoSomething(): void;
    }
}
```

As you can see, all of the type information is present but the implementation details have been left out. We will discuss these more in detail later when we start integrating other libraries such as jQuery.

The final compiler option allows us to pass a text file as the parameter to the compiler. This text file can contain the list of parameters for the compiler and all of the files for compilation, allowing us to bypass command line restrictions. This is the work-around to the buffer limit in the command line. In the following screenshot, you can see a text file that has been created to manage our compilation parameters:

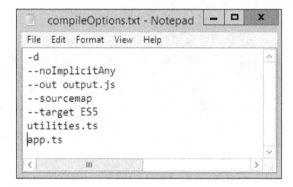

As you can see, we are now able to provide all of our parameters in an easily managed list. The following screenshot shows how to use this file with the compiler:

Summary

In this chapter, we covered each of the different parameters for the TypeScript compiler. We discussed how to target the different versions of ECMAScript as well as which external module pattern to follow. Source maps will become very handy to debug our TypeScript code and declaration files will help us deploy compiled JavaScript while still providing a rich type experience for developers using TypeScript. The ability to pass a file to the compiler allows us to create reusable compilation scripts that can scale much further than using the command line alone. Next, we are going to cover how the different constructs turn what is normally a scripting language into an object-oriented language.

4
Object-oriented Programming with TypeScript

Object-oriented Programming (OOP) is a concept built into many languages that help associate data and methods together in a single construct. Objects are created and are able to interact with each other using one another's public facing methods. JavaScript itself is not an object-oriented language in the way that C++, C#, or Java are. The construct of closures, which we discussed earlier allows us to bring object-oriented concepts into JavaScript development. TypeScript on the other hand can be treated as an object-oriented language because of the language constructs it introduces on top of JavaScript closures. In this chapter, we will discuss each of the core concepts behind object-oriented programming and how TypeScript allows JavaScript to implement this paradigm. The topics that will be covered in the chapter are as follows:

- SOLID
- Inheritance
- Encapsulation
- Abstraction
- Polymorphism

The basics

Before we dig into the main concepts of OOP, let's talk about what objects are and how they work. Objects are self-contained entities that maintain a set of data members and methods. The data members are unique to each object instance and the methods have direct access to these members. An object represents an instance of a class type and any number of instances can be created. Each of these instances will have different memory locations to store their internal member variables at runtime to differentiate between them. The following code sample shows a class definition and then the creation of different objects of that type:

```typescript
class Shape {
    public locationX: number = 0;
    public locationY: number = 0;
    public height: number = 0;
    public width: number = 0;
    constructor() {
    }
    public draw() {
    }
    public resize(height: number, width: number) {
        this.height = height;
        this.width = width;
    }
    public move(x: number, y: number) {
        this.locationX = x;
        this.locationY = y;
    }
}

var shapeInstance = new Shape();
var otherShape = new Shape();
shapeInstance.move(30, 35);
otherShape.resize(15, 15);
```

As you can see, we have a simple Shape class that contains a few data members as well as a few methods. We are then able to instantiate multiple instances of this class and store references to them so that we can operate on them separately. As you can see, we change the location of our first object and the size of the second object. If we were to access these members directly, shapeInstance would still have a height and width of 0 and location of (30, 35), while otherShape will still be located at (0, 0) with a height and width of 15.

SOLID – object-oriented design

SOLID is an acronym for five of the basic principles when designing classes in OOP. Following these principles will ensure that your application is well structured and flexible enough for the future. Let's take a look at what each of these letters represents:

- **Single Responsibility Principle**: A class should have only one reason to change. If a class has multiple responsibilities, then those responsibilities become coupled together. When this coupling occurs, it increases the potential for a change to one of the responsibilities to break the functionality of the other responsibilities. For more information on this principle, refer to: `http://www.objectmentor.com/resources/articles/srp.pdf`.

- **Open/Closed Principle**: An object should be open for extension but closed for modification. This principle is the basis for abstraction, which we will discuss briefly. Essentially, your programs should be designed around a specific set of contracts or abstract classes that should be extended to implement new functionality as requirements change. For more information on this principle, please refer to: `http://www.objectmentor.com/resources/articles/ocp.pdf`.

- **Liskov Substitution Principle**: An object should be able to be replaced with a subtype object without altering program execution. This principle builds on the Open/Closed Principle in that any subclass must maintain the minimum contract established by the base class. However, this principle goes a step further in that it applies to the client use of each object and the behavior expected from the base class. For more information on this principle, please refer to: `http://www.objectmentor.com/resources/articles/lsp.pdf`.

- **Interface Segregation Principle**: Many client specific interfaces are better than a single general purpose interface. This principle is important because it helps to decouple different behaviors from each other, allowing clients to only implement exactly what they need to. For more information on this principle, please refer to: `http://www.objectmentor.com/resources/articles/isp.pdf`.

- **Dependency Inversion Principle**: Rely on abstractions rather than concretions. This principle states that proper abstractions should be created that both dependent functions can rely on and concrete implementations will adhere to. When both are capable of using this abstraction, then it becomes simple to reuse code as requirements change with minimal impact. For more information on this principle, please refer to: `http://www.objectmentor.com/resources/articles/dip.pdf`.

Keeping these principles in mind while developing your applications will allow you to develop object-oriented code with the procedural language of JavaScript.

Understanding inheritance

Inheritance is the ability of a class to extend the functionality of an existing class. Inheritance creates a way for multiple objects to share a common core set of code and then extend or modify this as necessary for a specific purpose. Take for example our Shape class, which is very simple with a couple of properties in it, but these properties don't provide specific details as to what shape is actually being represented. In the following code, you can see we have modified the Shape class to be more generic and created a subclass using the extends construct in TypeScript:

```typescript
interface IShape {
    location: IPoint;
    move(newLocation: IPoint);
}
class Shape implements IShape {
    public location: IPoint = new Point(0, 0);
    constructor() {
    }
    public move(newLocation: IPoint) {
        this.location = newLocation;
    }
}
interface IRectangle extends IShape {
    height: number;
    width: number;
    area(): number;
    resize(height: number, width: number);
}
class Rectangle extends Shape implements IRectangle {
    public height: number = 0;
    public width: number = 0;
    constructor() {
        super();
    }
    public area(): number {
        return this.height * this.width;
    }
}
```

As you can see, we have a generic interface for the Shape class that implements only the basic functionality needed for a shape object, which is a location on a plane. The Point class is the same one we created back in *Chapter 2, TypeScript Basics*. Then a new interface gives us the properties and methods needed to define a basic rectangle shape. This interface is not explicitly necessary, but having it defined will allow us to extend or replace the Rectangle class easily in code later if we need to. This is followed by the class definition for a rectangle which, like the IRectangle definition, shows the usage of the extends keyword. This tells the compiler that the Rectangle class is a shape and should inherit all of the properties that come with it. Inside the constructor, an extra line must be added that initializes the base class instance.

 The call to the base class constructor must be the first statement inside the subclass constructor otherwise a compile-time error will occur.

Now every Rectangle object created will have not only the height, width, and area members but it will also contain a Location property and the Move method that are defined by the Shape class. This is not a default construct in the language of JavaScript so let's take a quick look at the output provided by the compiler to see how this is implemented:

```
var __extends = this.__extends || function (d, b) {
    for (var p in b) if (b.hasOwnProperty(p)) d[p] = b[p];
    function __() { this.constructor = d; }
    __.prototype = b.prototype;
    d.prototype = new __();
};
var Point = (function () {
    function Point(x, y) {
        if (typeof x === "undefined") { x = 0; }
        if (typeof y === "undefined") { y = 0; }
        this.x = x;
        this.y = y;
    }
    return Point;
})();

var Shape = (function () {
```

```
      function Shape() {
          this.location = new Point(0, 0);
      }
      Shape.prototype.move = function (newLocation) {
          this.location = newLocation;
      };
      return Shape;
  })();

  var Rectangle = (function (_super) {
      __extends(Rectangle, _super);
      function Rectangle() {
          _super.call(this);
          this.height = 0;
          this.width = 0;
      }
      Rectangle.prototype.area = function () {
          return this.height * this.width;
      };
      return Rectangle;
  })(Shape);
```

As you can see, all of our classes are created as modules as discussed previously, but before any of these are generated, the compiler injects a special segment of code to handle extending classes. The TypeScript compiler implements object-oriented principles for us by applying a standard set of well-known patterns—member addition and prototype copying. This code takes in two object types as parameters. The first parameter is the subclass that is in need of all of the base class's properties, and the second is the base class itself. This function then loops through each of the available members on the base class and adds them to the subclass. Then the prototype of the base class is copied onto the subclass's prototype. When we look at the module that is output for the subclass, you can see that the Shape type is passed to the Rectangle's module definition for use in the newly generated function. The first thing that happens in the Rectangle's type definition is that it makes a call to this newly generated extends function and then proceeds to initialize the Rectangle as it normally would. The final piece of this is the call to initialize a new Shape object using the call method and passing in the current object instance. This tells the Shape constructor to perform all of its operations on the current object rather than initializing a new object.

TypeScript, like most object-oriented languages, only allows for single inheritance when defining a class. So, creating two classes that perform different functions and then attempting to merge them with a single subclass is not possible and a compile error will be generated. This is very different from the way interfaces work but it is necessary because it would be impossible to ensure proper functionality in all scenarios where this could occur. These two separate classes could define properties or methods with similar names and call signatures and the subclass would have no way of differentiating between them. If you find yourself in a scenario where this is needed, you should consider refactoring your code.

While multiple inheritance is not possible for a single class, we are able to chain a series of classes together to merge functionality in this manner. In the next example, we create a new interface called IBox to define the new requirements for a box object. This interface will extend the IRectangle interface to merge their definitions. The concrete implementation of IBox will inherit from the Rectangle class we created earlier to bring its methods and properties on to the Box class. This creates an inheritance tree stemming from the basic Shape class we created initially, to the Rectangle object, and finally into the Box class, as you can see in the following example:

```
interface IBox extends IRectangle {
    depth: number;
}
class Box extends Rectangle implements IBox {
    public depth: number = 0;
    constructor() {
        super();
    }
    public resize(height: number, width: number, depth: number) {
        super.resize(height, width);
        this.depth = depth;
    }
}
```

An extra property is added to the IBox interface, representing a three-dimensional object and all of the functionality of both Shape and Rectangle is available. The resize method has been modified to take an extra parameter that will allow us to modify the new property. There is a problem with this example though; it is in violation of one of the SOLID principles that we discussed earlier. Attempting to compile this code will result in an incompatible type error because the resize method of Rectangle has a different call signature than Box's implementation of it. To fix this, change the resize method to the following:

```
public resize(height: number, width: number, depth: number = 0) {
    super.resize(height, width);
    this.depth = depth;
}
```

This parameter must be optional, otherwise we risk breaking the Liskov Substitution Principle that we discussed earlier in this chapter; however, we want to ensure it has a valid value if it is not provided to the constructor. For this reason, the depth parameter is given an initializer rather than just making it optional: `depth?: number`. If this parameter was not optional, then we would receive compilation errors if we changed any Rectangle object in our application to a `Box`, as shown in the following code sample:

```
//var rect = new Rectangle();
var rect = new Box();
rect.resize(4, 3);
```

Now that we've started to create a complex object tree, let's take a look at the relationships between the different classes we have so far. The following diagram lays out the **Is-a** and **Has-a** relationship between all of our different objects:

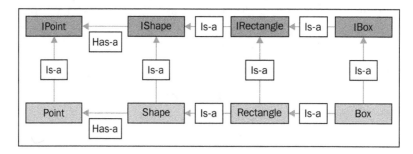

As you can see, just these few simple classes and interfaces can create a very complex object tree. As applications grow, this can become harder and harder to manage, however if you follow the guidelines for developing object-oriented code, you will be able to maintain your applications with relative ease.

Encapsulation

The concept of encapsulation in OOP allows us to define all of the necessary members for an object to function while hiding the internal implementation details from the application using the object. This is a very powerful concept for us to use because it allows us to change the internal workings of a class without breaking any of its dependent objects. This could come in the form of either private members or private method implementations. The contract that has been established remains the same and the functionality that it provides is consistent, however, improvements are able to be made. In the following code segment, you can see how hiding certain members from the calling application will be beneficial:

```
interface IActivator {
```

```
    activateLicense(): boolean;
}
class LocalActivator implements IActivator {
    private _remainingLicenses: number = 5;
    constructor() {
    }
    public activateLicense(): boolean {
        this._remainingLicenses--;
        if (this._remainingLicenses > 0)
            return true;
        throw "Out of Licenses";
    }
}
```

In this example, we have an interface that defines a type that will manage the activation of licenses for a product. This is followed by a concrete implementation of the interface that locally keeps track of the remaining licenses and returns a true value if there are remaining licenses, otherwise an exception is thrown to stop program execution. The number of licenses is kept in a private variable so that the calling application can't give itself more licenses to work with. In real-world scenarios, however, the actual implementation details would likely make a call to a server that determines whether the product has licenses remaining. Thanks to encapsulation, we could change the implementation details of this class too without the client ever knowing the difference, other than the delay in making a server request. In the following code segment, you can see how we are able to swap the LocalActivator object with a ServerActivator object and program execution continues to function as expected:

```
class ServerActivator implements IActivator {
    constructor() {
    }
    public activateLicense(): boolean {
        var request = new XMLHttpRequest();
        var requestResponse: boolean = false;
        request.open('GET', '/license/activate', false);

        request.onload = () => {
            if (request.status == 200) {
                requestResponse = true;
            } else {
                throw "An error occured during activation!";
            }
        };

        request.onerror = () => {
```

```
                throw "An error occured during activation!";
            }
            request.send(null);
            return requestResponse;
        }
    }
//var activator: IActivator = new LocalActivator();
var activator: IActivator = new ServerActivator();
var isActive = activator.activateLicense();
if (isActive) {
    //Program logic
}
```

The `ServerActivator` class implements the same interface as `LocalActivator` we declared earlier, but it makes a synchronous request back to the server for data rather than doing it on the client. Normally, this type of request should be made asynchronously, however, we would need to change the `IActivator` interface to support promises or use callbacks.

Promises will be natively supported in ECMAScript 6, however several libraries have implemented their own implementation. More information on ECMAScript 6 promises can be found here at: `http://www.html5rocks.com/en/tutorials/es6/promises/`.

The implementation details between the two objects is vastly different but the end result is the same. The two can be used interchangeably and the application requires no further changes.

Abstraction

Abstraction is an incredibly powerful concept in object-oriented development. It encompasses the idea of hiding specific implementation details while providing the high-level definition of what should be implemented. In the previous example, we saw a very basic case of abstraction. The `IActivator` interface creates the abstraction layer needed to handle the concept of activating the application. The `LocalActivator` and `ServerActivator` types are concrete implementations of this abstraction. In other programming languages such as C#, classes are able to declare specific members as abstract. This forces any subclasses of the base type to provide a concrete implementation of that member. In the following code segment, you will see a C# example of this:

```
public abstract class AbstractBaseClass
{
```

```
    protected bool isActive = false;
    public AbstractBaseClass()
    {
    }
    public abstract bool CheckStatus();
}
public class ConcreteClass : AbstractBaseClass
{
    public ConcreteClass()
    {
    }
    public override bool CheckStatus()
    {
        return this.isActive;
    }
}
```

The base class provides the declaration for a method called CheckStatus, however, no implementation is provided. The implementation is forced upon the ConcreteClass type, however, members made available in the base class are available to this implementation. The abstract keyword on the CheckStatus method tells the compiler that all subclasses of the AbstractBaseClass must implement this method or a compile error will be generated. The abstract keyword on the AbstractBaseClass will cause the compiler to generate an error if the class is instantiated directly. The simplest way to do this in TypeScript is through the use of interfaces, however, this does not provide the full functionality that comes from abstract classes in C#. The protected member in the base class is not accessible outside of the concrete implementations of the type, however if it is placed on a TypeScript interface, then it must be made publicly available. Despite the lack of an abstract keyword and language construct in TypeScript, we can use certain patterns to create a similar implementation:

```
class AbstractClass {
    constructor() {
    }
    public checkStatus(): boolean {
        throw new Error("Not Implemented");";
    }
}
class ConcreteClass extends AbstractClass {
    private _isActive: boolean = false;
    constructor() {
        super();
    }
```

```
    public checkStatus(): boolean {
        return this._isActive;
    }
}
```

As you can see, we must still define a complete class that represents the abstract base class. However, in the method implementation of `checkStatus`, an exception is thrown at runtime that will stop program execution whenever an attempt to use this class directly is made. It would be nice if there was some way to enforce this at compile time, however, currently this functionality does not exist. TypeScript does not have a protected accessibility level so we have been forced to move this detail down into the concrete class explicitly. In this specific case, it would make sense to just make the `AbstractClass` into an interface that the `ConcreteClass` type would then implement; however, as our objects become more complex, we will want to have publicly accessible members that are defined only once in the base type and specific method implementations will need to be provided by the concrete classes.

Polymorphism

Polymorphism in its pure definition means to have many shapes. When this is applied to software development, it applies to a wide variety of techniques that enable us to use a variety of different objects or methods to perform a task. In pure OOP languages, polymorphism refers to the use of method overloading, operator overloading, and method overriding.

Method overloading

Method overloading is the idea of providing multiple methods with different call signatures but the same name. We discussed this earlier in *Chapter 2, TypeScript Basics*, so this will be a short review of that. As we saw earlier, we are able to provide multiple call signatures for a single function as long as the parameters all share a common base type. The ICommunicator interface shown in the following code provides an example of this:

```
interface ICommunicator {
    speak(message: string);
    speak(message: number);
    sipeak(message: boolean);
    speak(message: any);
}
class Communicator implements ICommunicator {
    constructor() {
    }
    speak(message: string);
```

```
        speak(message: number);
        speak(message: boolean);
        speak(message: any) {
            alert(message);
        }
    }
```

In this example, we defined a class that is used for communicating messages. The message can be of any of the types defined in the method list, and they all share a common base type that must be used in the final method signature, as discussed in *Chapter 2, TypeScript Basics*. In traditional object-oriented languages, we would be able to define multiple implementations of the `speak` method, however since the end result is still plain JavaScript, we can only provide the single method block. Through the use of conditional statements, we could provide different execution paths for each of the different types used in the parameter list, as shown in the following example:

```
class Communicator implements ICommunicator {
    constructor() {
    }
    speak(message: string);
    speak(message: number);
    speak(message: boolean);
    speak(message: any) {
        if (typeof message === "string") {
            alert(message);
        } else if (typeof message === "number") {
            alert("The number provided was: " + message);
        } else if (typeof message === "boolean") {
            alert("The boolean value was: " + message);
        } else {
            alert(message);
        }
    }
}
```

Operator overloading

JavaScript is not inherently an object-oriented language and this limits what we can do somewhat, so we are still restricted in some respects compared to languages such as C#. There is no way to perform operator overloading in JavaScript so we are forced to implement specific methods on our classes to implement the functionality we want. In the following example, we defined a `Vector` type that will allow us to perform vector math operations:

```
interface IVector {
```

```
        x: number;
        y: number;
}
class Vector implements IVector {
        public x: number = 0;
        public y: number = 0;
        constructor(x = 0, y = 0) {
                this.x = x;
                this.y = y;
        }
}
```

We know that performing vector addition is fairly simple so it would be very nice if we could use the + operator to add two instances of this class together.

```
var v1 = new Vector(2, 5);
var v2 = new Vector(4, 3);
var v3 = v1 + v2;
alert(v3);
```

However, since operator overloading is not available in JavaScript, the result will end up looking something similar to the following screenshot:

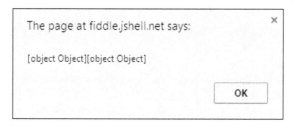

Behind the scenes, the JavaScript engine calls the toString method associated with the objects and then concatenates them into a single value. This has the potential to cause unexpected results in our applications. To perform the functionality we want, we must explicitly implement methods to handle the desired functionality.

```
public add(v: IVector): IVector {
        var newVector = new Vector();
        newVector.x = this.x + v.x;
        newVector.y = this.y + v.y;
        return newVector;
}
public static add(v1: IVector, v2: IVector): IVector {
```

```
        return v1.add(v2);
    }
```

After adding these methods to our class definition and performing a method override of `toString`, we can simply change our application code to call the new `add` method and we will receive the expected result:

```
var v3 = Vector.add(v1, v2);
alert("X: " + v3.x + ", Y: " + v3.y);
```

The end result will now be a new `Vector` object that is the sum of the two vectors:

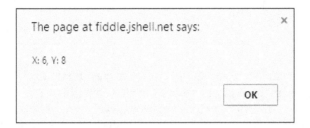

Method overrides

Method overrides are a way to replace functionality that is inherited from super-classes. Method overrides must have the same call signature as the method that is being overridden. Take a look at the following example:

```
interface IEmployee {
    name: string;
    email: string;
    work(tasks: string[]);
}
class Employee implements IEmployee {
    constructor(public name: string, public email: string) {
    }
    public work(tasks: string[]) {
        for (var i = 0; i < tasks.length; i++) {
            //perform task
        }
    }
}
interface IManager extends IEmployee {
    employees: IEmployee[];
}
```

```typescript
class Manager extends Employee implements IManager {
    public employees: IEmployee[] = [];
    constructor(name: string, email: string, employees: IEmployee[]) {
        super(name, email);
        this.employees = employees;
    }
    public work(tasks: string[]) {
        for (var i = 0; i < this.employees.length; i++) {
            for (var j = 0; j < tasks.length; j++) {
                this.employees[i].work([tasks[j]]);
            }
        }
    }
}
```

In this example, you can see that we have two classes. First, a generic `Employee` class that represents the base class for any employee within an organization. This employee has a few properties such as a name and an e-mail address to contact them with. Then, second, there is a very simple method that allows the employee to be passed a list of tasks, and this task list will be executed sequentially until all of the tasks are complete. The next class is the `Manager` class, which is a subclass of `Employee`. The manager has all of the same functions as a normal employee, they just also have a list of employees that they are responsible for. The manager is handed a list of tasks, and rather than performing each one explicitly, it will delegate each task to each of its employees for execution. If we were to add or remove parameters from the `Work` method, then the call signatures would be different between the subclass and superclass and would break the Liskov substitution principle. TypeScript will not stop you from changing the method signature, however, it will make your code harder to manage.

References

To find out more about object-oriented design and object-oriented programming concepts, visit:

- http://www.objectmentor.com/omSolutions/oops_what.html
- http://www.codeproject.com/Articles/22769/Introduction-to-Object-Oriented-Programming-Concep

Summary

Throughout this chapter, you should have gained a basic understanding of object-oriented programming. We have looked at several examples of how to put the encapsulation, polymorphism, abstraction, and inheritance into practice and how they allow us to make scalable applications. The SOLID principles helped us to outline how our classes should be designed. We are now going to put these concepts into use over the next few chapters. We will be developing an interactive drawing application with TypeScript and a little bit of HTML in *Chapter 5, Creating a Simple Drawing Application*.

5
Creating a Simple Drawing Application

We have covered a lot of information in a very short period of time. Let's take that information and put it to use; let's build a full application rather than just looking at code samples. We are going to build a web-based drawing application similar to Paint, but it will be hosted in the browser. The topics we will cover in this chapter include:

- Creating the project
- Basic shapes
- Drawing objects on the canvas
- Managing the canvas state and decision making
- Keeping track of the application state

Setting up the project

First things first, we need to create a new project that will host our application and configure the compiler settings. Create a new project in Visual Studio, using the TypeScript project template as described in *Chapter 2, TypeScript Basics*, and call it DrawingApplication. Then, open up the project properties by right-clicking on the project and selecting **Properties**.

In the following screenshot, you can see the settings we will use for this application:

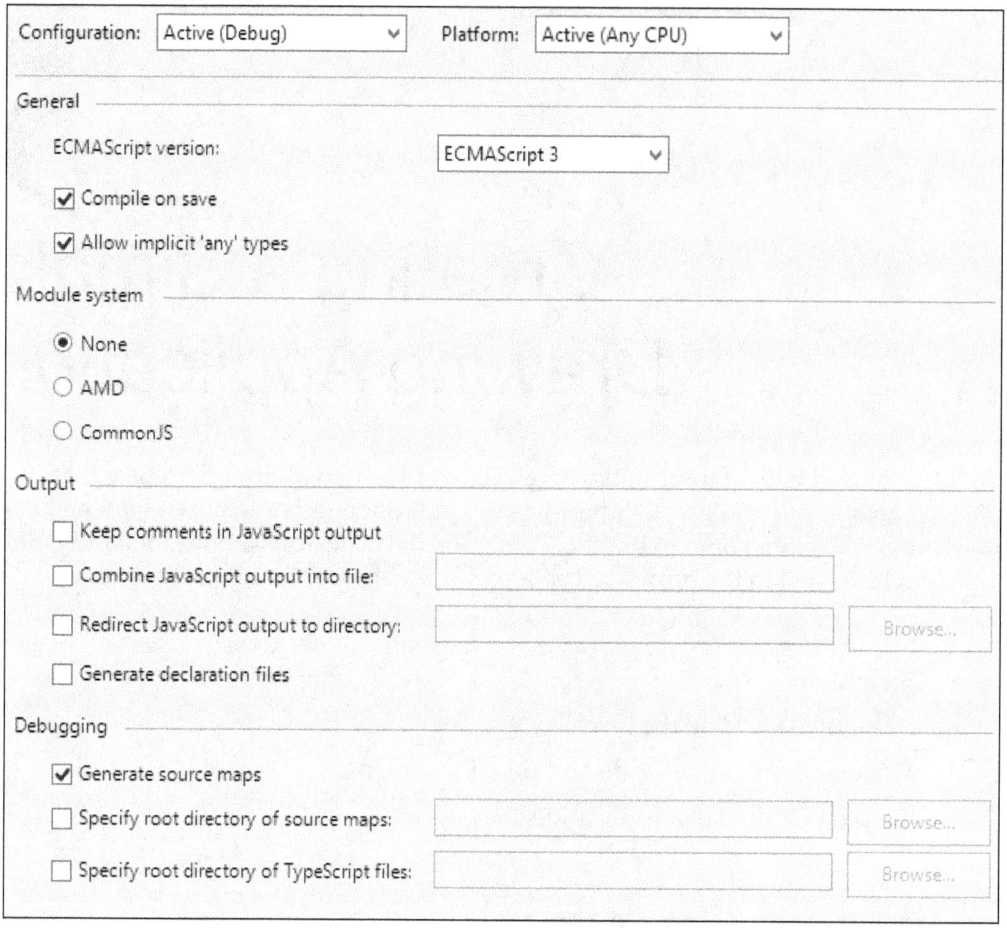

As you can see, we will be targeting ECMAScript 3 to ensure a broader scope of platforms that our application will run on. We will not be using an external module system, comments will be removed from the final output, and the rest of the output can be left as the default values. Next, we need to modify index.html to contain a canvas element. The HTML canvas element is part of the HTML5 standard, which is supported by most modern browsers at this point. Since we aren't using jQuery yet, we will also need to move the loading of our app.js file to within the body; that way, the canvas element will be available to us at runtime. The following screenshot shows the index.html file after making these modifications:

```
index.html  ⇥  ✕  app.ts
    <!DOCTYPE html>
    <html lang="en">
    <head>
        <meta charset="utf-8" />
        <title>TypeScript HTML App</title>
        <link rel="stylesheet" href="app.css" type="text/css" />
    </head>
    <body>
        <h1>Drawing Application</h1>
        <div id="content">
            <canvas id="drawingCanvas" height="600" width="900"/>
        </div>
        <script src="app.js"></script>
    </body>
    </html>
```

Now that we have the basics for the project set up, let's start putting together an object-oriented TypeScript application. As we move through this chapter, we will use a couple of enumerations to help us define abstractions and allow our types to communicate in a strongly typed fashion. I prefer to maintain a clear separation of code for easy navigation, so all of the enums that are created will be placed in a file called Enums.ts. The two enums are as follows:

```
enum DrawingToolType {
    Select,
    Rectangle,
    Circle,
    Line,
    Freehand
}
enum CanvasEngineAction {
    None,
    Move,
    Resize
}
```

The DrawingToolType type will be used to help determine which drawing tool the user has selected. The type responsible for interacting with the canvas will need to know this to function properly. The CanvasEngineAction type will be used by the objects responsible for drawing the shapes to inform the canvas operator what to do with the user's input.

The shapes

In keeping with the principles that we learned in the previous chapter, we will need a variety of different types to perform different tasks within our application. We will need a representation of what shapes are, how to draw them, something to interact with the user interface, and somewhere to maintain the list of objects to be drawn.

Basic shapes

The first thing we need is a set of classes that will represent the different shapes that we eventually intend on drawing. These objects should be kept separate from the drawing logic that we will implement later. The first thing we need to do is create an abstraction for each of the shapes we intend on representing. This abstraction will allow us to easily extend object types or swap certain objects for others as requirements change. The abstraction is as follows:

```
interface IPoint {
    x: number;
    y: number;
}
interface IShape {
}
interface IRectangle extends IShape {
    height: number;
    width: number;
    resize(height: number, width: number);
}
interface ICircle extends IShape {
    radius: number;
    resize(radius: number);
    area(): number;
}
interface ILine extends IShape {
    p1: IPoint;
    p2: IPoint;
    length(): number;
}
interface IFreehand extends IShape {
    points: Array<IPoint>;
    addPoint(point: IPoint);
}
```

As you can see, we have several basic shape interfaces that handle the properties associated with the specific type of shape. The IShape interface is empty for now, but having it provides a common base type for all shapes we create. In the next code sample, the concrete implementation of each of our shape interfaces is shown. These types can be reused across any number of applications that require the representation of shapes and are therefore more useful than if they had been coupled directly to the drawing logic:

```
class Point implements IPoint {
    constructor(public x: number, public y: number) {
    }
}
class Rectangle implements IRectangle {
    constructor(public height: number, public width: number) {
    }
    public resize(height: number, width: number) {
        this.height = height;
        this.width = width;
    }
}
class Circle implements ICircle {
    constructor(public radius: number) {
    }
    public resize(radius: number) {
        this.radius = radius;
    }
    public area(): number {
        return Math.PI * this.radius * this.radius;
    }
}
class Line implements ILine {
    constructor(public p1: IPoint, public p2: IPoint) {
    }
    public length(): number {
        var a2 = Math.pow(this.p2.x - this.p1.x, 2);
        var b2 = Math.pow(this.p2.y - this.p1.y, 2);
        return Math.sqrt(a2 + b2);
    }
}
class Freehand implements IFreehand {
    public points: Array<IPoint> = [];
```

```
    constructor() {
    }
    public addPoint(point: IPoint) {
        this.points.push(point);
    }
}
```

Each of these classes is limited to a single responsibility that keeps track of the shape's state and reports the various properties associated with it. All of this functionality is useful, but it doesn't get us fully to our goal of having objects drawn on the canvas.

Drawing shapes

Now that we have the basic representation of what we want to draw, we need to define objects that will handle this. These objects should do the least amount of work required to draw the shapes they represent. This means no direct interaction with the **Document Object Model (DOM)**. The following interfaces represent the different abstractions that we will use to represent a shape that can be drawn and manipulated on the canvas element:

```
interface IDraw {
    draw(ctx: CanvasRenderingContext2D);
}
interface IResize {
    inResizeZone: (mouse: IPoint) => boolean;
    resizeToLocation: (to: IPoint) => void;
}
interface IMove {
    move: (to: IPoint) => void;
    contains: (mousePoint: IPoint, ctx: CanvasRenderingContext2D) =>
boolean;
    getMoveOffset(mousePos: IPoint): IPoint;
}
interface IDrawingShape extends IDraw, IResize, IMove {
    shape: IShape;
    location: IPoint;
    isSelected: boolean;
    selectionZoneWidth: number;
    opacity: number;
    getCursorType: (mousePoint: IPoint) => string;
    getClickLocationAction(mouse: IPoint, ctx:
CanvasRenderingContext2D): CanvasEngineAction;
}
```

Each of these interfaces could easily be combined into a single interface, but in accordance with the interface segregation principle, each of these actions can now be decoupled from one another if needs be. The IDrawingShape interface eventually merges each of these types while adding some of its own functionality. All of this put together represents a type that we will be able to draw on the HTML canvas element and interact with in some way. Each IDrawingShape instance holds a reference to its specific shape that can then be accessed or manipulated by our application logic. Separating each shape from the drawing-specific interface upholds the single responsibility principle by allowing the shape to keep track of its data while the drawing objects will only be responsible for methods related to rendering the specific shape in the browser. The shape's location on the canvas is managed by the drawing shape as well as whether it is the currently selected object on the canvas. The getCursorType and getClickLocationAction functions are application-specific and will allow the object responsible for handling user interaction to request information from the drawing objects before proceeding through its application logic. The concrete implementation of this interface is as follows:

```
class DrawingShapeBase implements IDrawingShape {
    public shape: IShape = null;
    public location: IPoint = new Point(0, 0);
    public isSelected: boolean = false;
    public selectionZoneWidth: number = 4;
    public opacity: number = 1;
    constructor() {
    }
    public inResizeZone(mouse: IPoint): boolean {
        throw "Method not implemented";
    }
    public move(to: IPoint) {
        this.location = to;
    }
    public resizeToLocation(to: IPoint) {
        throw "Method not implemented";
    }
    public contains(mousePoint: IPoint, ctx:
CanvasRenderingContext2D): boolean {
        throw "Method not implemented";
    }
    public draw(ctx: CanvasRenderingContext2D) {
        throw "Method not implemented";
    }
    public getMoveOffset(mousePos: IPoint): IPoint {
```

```
            return new Point(0, 0);
        }
    public getCursorType(mousePoint: IPoint): string {
        throw "Method not implemented";
    }
    public getClickLocationAction(mousePoint: Point, ctx:
CanvasRenderingContext2D): CanvasEngineAction {
            if (this.inResizeZone(mousePoint)) {
                return CanvasEngineAction.Resize;
            }
            else if (this.contains(mousePoint, ctx)) {
                return CanvasEngineAction.Drag;
            }
            return CanvasEngineAction.None;
        }
    }
```

As you can see, this is a very simple base class and is not meant to be instantiated directly. It provides a few default implementations that can be reused by shapes if necessary but are also available to be overloaded. So, now we have our shape abstractions set up, let's start implementing the specific logic for each of the different shapes we intend on drawing in our application. The following screenshot shows a concrete implementation of the DrawingShape type specifically for the Rectangle shape that we defined earlier:

```
class DrawingRectangle extends DrawingShapeBase implements IFillStyle {
    public shape: IRectangle = new Rectangle(0, 0);
    public fillStyle: string = "#FF0000"
    constructor() ...
    public inResizeZone(point: IPoint): boolean ...
    public resizeToLocation(to: IPoint) ...
    public draw(ctx: CanvasRenderingContext2D) ...
    public contains(mousePoint: IPoint, context: CanvasRenderingContext2D): boolean ...
    public getMoveOffset(mousePosition: IPoint): IPoint ...
    public getCursorType(mousePoint: IPoint) ...
}
```

We will go over the specific implementations of each of the different methods when we come across their use. The full code is available online. For now, let's just look at the most basic thing we are trying to do, which is to draw a rectangle on the canvas:

```
public draw(ctx: CanvasRenderingContext2D) {
        ctx.fillStyle = "#FF0000";
        ctx.globalAlpha = this.Opacity;
```

```
        ctx.fillRect(this.location.x, this.location.y, this.shape.
width, this.shape.height);
        ctx.strokeStyle = "#000000";
        ctx.lineWidth = 3;
        ctx.strokeRect(this.location.x, this.location.y, this.shape.
width, this.shape.height);
    }
```

As we defined earlier in the abstraction of our types, the `Draw` method takes in one parameter which is of type `CanvasRenderingContext2D`. This type is a description of the object returned by the canvas element that allows us to draw our different objects directly on the canvas. The rectangle is very easy to draw using the context object's API.

 The HTML5 canvas object has a very robust API; for the full list of what it is capable of, visit `http://www.w3schools.com/ tags/ref_canvas.asp`.

The first thing we do is set the color that we want our rectangle to be; this must be done using RGB hex triplets. We can then send the transparency level that the object will be using the `globalAlpha` property. Next, we use the context to render the rectangle on the canvas object using the properties of the shape object and the drawing object's location. We are also going to display a border around the rectangle, so we set the stroke color in the same fashion, followed by the width of the border that we want to draw. Then, once again, we call upon the context to render the object we want on the canvas. OK, we now have a shape type and a type that can render it in the browser. Let's create a shape and test the application:

```
var canvas = <HTMLCanvasElement>window.document.getElementById("drawi
ngCanvas");
var ctx = canvas.getContext("2d");
var shape1 = new DrawingRectangle();
shape1.move(new Point(20, 60));
shape1.shape.resize(60, 80);
shape1.draw(ctx);
```

First we grab the canvas from the DOM and cast it to the `HTMLCanvasElement` type so that we can easily access its different properties. We need to get the rendering context that will be used by our drawing objects to display their shapes. Then, we create a new `DrawingRectangle` and move it to a new location and give it a size. Finally, we tell the shape to draw itself using the context object for our canvas element.

In the following screenshot, you can see that we have a red rectangle with a black border around it. It is positioned 20 pixels from the left edge and 60 pixels down from the top edge. The top-left edge of the canvas represents the origin, or Point(0, 0).

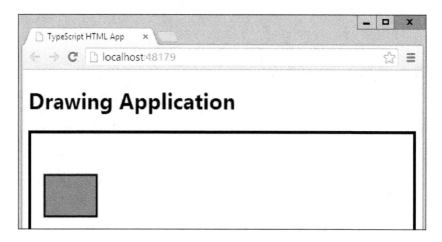

Now that we can draw the shape on the canvas, let's define how it can be manipulated. The remainder of the work is done by calculations based on the shape type that is being represented and the actions performed by the user. The Move functionality was provided by the base type because it doesn't require any interaction with the shape directly. Any subclass that wants to manipulate how the Move method works can override it, as we learned in *Chapter 4, Object-oriented Programming with TypeScript*. Next, let's take a look at the methods for resizing DrawingRectangle:

```
public inResizeZone(point: IPoint): boolean {
    return ((point.X >= this.location.x + this.shape.width - this.
selectionZoneWidth &&
        point.x <= this.location.x + this.shape.width + this.
selectionZoneWidth) &&
        (point.y >= this.location.y + this.shape.height - this.
selectionZoneWidth &&
        point.y <= this.location.y + this.shape.height + this.
selectionZoneWidth));
}
public resizeToLocation(to: IPoint) {
    var cursor = window.document.body.style.cursor;
    if (cursor == "se-resize") {
        this.shape.width = to.x - this.location.x;
        this.shape.height = to.y - this.location.y;
    }
}
```

The first method determines whether the point parameter resides within the boundaries of the selection zone for the drawing object. It will be used to help the engine we build in the next section make decisions. For DrawingRectangle, this is the bottom-right corner; however, hovering over exactly the right pixel to manage this is fairly difficult. This is why there is a selection zone with a configurable size. The ResizeToLocation method takes in a point and modifies the properties of the underlying shape object to resize it. For the rectangle, this is as simple as taking the difference between the incoming point and the current location of the rectangle. The other methods of the abstraction are shown in the following code. They are used to provide information to the canvas engine so that it can appropriately interact with the user.

```
public contains(mousePoint: IPoint, context:
CanvasRenderingContext2D): boolean {
    if (this.shape.height < 0) {
        this.location.y = this.location.y + this.shape.height;
        this.shape.height = this.shape.height * -1;
    }
    if (this.shape.width < 0) {
        this.location.x = this.location.x + this.shape.width;
        this.shape.width = this.shape.width * -1;
    }
    return (this.location.x <= mousePoint.x) &&
        (this.location.x + this.shape.width >= mousePoint.x) &&
        (this.location.y <= mousePoint.y) &&
        (this.location.y + this.shape.height >= mousePoint.y);
}
public getMoveOffset(mousePosition: IPoint): IPoint {
    return new Point(mousePosition.x - this.location.x,
mousePosition.y - this.location.y);
}
public getCursorType(mousePoint: IPoint) {
    if (this.inResizeZone(mousePoint))
        return "se-resize";
    else
        return "move";
}
```

The contains method does a little bit of maintenance on the state of the shape to ensure it performs the correct calculations. If the height or width of the rectangle is less than zero, then the logic to determine whether the provided point is within the bounds of the shape will not perform as expected. getMoveOffset returns the x and y offsets needed to provide a smooth dragging experience across the canvas. The last piece of the puzzle is the getCursorType method, which tells the engine to inform the user that this region is interactive by changing the cursor.

Making the application interactive

Now we have the ability to make any number of shapes and present them to the user. This, however, is very limited in functionality and doesn't allow for any interaction between the application and the consumer. Most drawing applications allow for basic movement and resizing of the objects on the canvas. This requires the application to redraw itself each time the user attempts to change one of the shapes.

The engine

To handle the drawing and updating of the canvas state, we will need a new type that is focused around maintaining this. This type, which we'll call `CanvasEngine`, should have a very simple abstraction since it only needs to perform a few basic tasks: drawing the canvas, clearing the canvas, and receiving requests to redraw the current frame:

```
interface ICanvasEngine {
    invalidate();
    clear();
    draw();
}
```

The object will do more under the covers, but any object consuming the engine needs only these functions to interact with it. Now let's take a look at the more complex implementation of this type. In the following screenshot, you can see the full implementation. This will be followed by a breakdown of each public and private method.

```
class CanvasEngine implements ICanvasEngine {
    private context: CanvasRenderingContext2D;
    private action: CanvasEngineAction = CanvasEngineAction.None;
    private _dragOffsetX: number = 0;
    private _dragOffsetY: number = 0;
    constructor(private _canvas: HTMLCanvasElement, private _model: IDrawingModel) [...]
    public clear() [...]
    public invalidate() [...]
    public draw() [...]
    //#region Private
    private _getMousePosition(canvas: HTMLCanvasElement, e: MouseEvent): IPoint [...]
    private _setShapeAsSelected(shape: IDrawingShape) [...]
    private _clearEngineState() [...]
    private _bringToFront(index: number) [...]
    private _mousedown(e) [...]
    private _mousemove(e) [...]
    private _mouseup(e) [...]
    //#endregion Private
}
```

As you can see, we have a number of private methods and event handlers that will help us interpret user actions. The constructor takes in the canvas we want to work with and a model that is responsible for maintaining a list of shapes for the engine to operate on. This model has been abstracted the same way the rest of our types have to maintain a decoupled application.

```
interface IDrawingModel {
    selection: IDrawingShape;
    shapes: IDrawingShape[];
    addShape(shape: IDrawingShape);
    getNewShape(location: IPoint): IDrawingShape;
    getDrawingTool(): DrawingToolType;
}
```

We will look at the concrete implementation of this type later, but knowing what the interface is will allow us to proceed with the engine code. We will start in the constructor, then move on to the `public` methods, and finally look at the private user interaction focused methods. As you can see in the following code sample, the constructor does a few things to set up not only the engine's state, but also to wire up the event handlers:

```
constructor(private _canvas: HTMLCanvasElement, private _model:
IDrawingModel) {
        this.ctx = this._canvas.getContext("2d");
        this._canvas.addEventListener('mousedown', (e) => this._
mousedown(e), true);
        this._canvas.addEventListener('mousemove', (e) => this._
mousemove(e), true);
        this._canvas.addEventListener('mouseup', (e) => this._
mouseup(e), true);
    }
```

The first thing we do is get the rendering context that we will use to manipulate the canvas. This is stored as a private variable and will be used throughout the application's life cycle. The next thing we do is wire up the event handlers to the canvas element. We need to perform specific actions as the user manipulates objects on the canvas with the mouse. The syntax for directing the events towards our private methods looks a little strange though. This is not valid JavaScript code, but when it gets compiled it will run just fine. The `=>` syntax inside of the constructor tells the TypeScript compiler to generate a special representation to the `this` object in the final JavaScript representation. The final JavaScript code will look something similar to the following:

```
function CanvasEngine(_canvas, _model) {
        var _this = this;
```

```
this._canvas.addEventListener('mousedown', function (e) {
        return _this._mousedown(e);
    }, true);
}
```

This ensures that when the event listener we are attaching to the canvas is called, we have a correct reference to the engine's instance. Otherwise, we could end up using a `this` object that doesn't represent the `CanvasEngine` instance; in this case, the DOM element that fired the event and the call to the `_mousedown` method would fail. Now that we have our object being instantiated and events being wired up, let's take a look at the public methods. The `Clear` and `Invalidate` methods are both very simple:

```
public clear() {
    this.ctx.clearRect(0, 0, this._canvas.width, this._canvas.height);
}
public invalidate() {
    window.requestAnimationFrame(() => this.draw());
}
```

The `clear` method overwrites the entire canvas with a blank rectangle to remove all existing objects from view. The `invalidate` method makes a call to the `draw` method to show all of the objects represented by the drawing model that was passed in to the constructor. The `draw` method isn't much more complex than either of these methods because of the drawing shape abstractions we made earlier.

```
public Draw() {
    var shapes: Array<IDraw> = this._model.shapes;
    this.clear();
    if (shapes) {
        for (var i = 0; i < shapes.length; i++) {
            this.context.save();
            shapes[i].draw(this.context);
            this.context.restore();
        }
    }
}
```

In this method, we get a reference to each of the shapes the model wants us to draw and clear the canvas of any existing drawings. We then loop through the list of shapes and have each one draw its shape. Since we abstracted the drawing interface away, the actual type of each object is irrelevant to the engine as long as it implements the `draw` method. As you can see, we wrapped the call to the draw method in two calls to the context object: `save` and `restore`.

These methods are used to persist the context's drawing state from before the specific drawing shape changes it and revert to this state after it completes. With these methods alone, we have created a way to repeatedly draw frames on the canvas. Combined with the following implementation of the `IDrawingModel` interface we saw earlier, we can effectively simulate objects moving across the screen:

```
class DrawingModel implements IDrawingModel {
    public selection: IDrawingShape = null;
    public shapes: IDrawingShape[] = [];
    constructor() {
    }
    public addShape(shape: IDrawingShape) {
        this.shapes.push(shape);
    }
    public getNewShape(location: IPoint): IDrawingShape {
        throw ("Not implemented");
    }
    public getDrawingTool(): DrawingToolType {
        return DrawingToolType.Select;
    }
}
```

This is the bare minimum for this class and we will fill in the `getNewShape` and `getDrawingTool` methods later. For now though, we can store a list of shapes and add new shapes to this list and the canvas will be able to redraw them for us. If we modify our application code from the previous example to create a `DrawingModel` and add our shape to it, then we can code to manipulate our rectangle and have it move across the screen.

```
var model: IDrawingModel = new DrawingModel();
model.addShape(shape1);
var engine: ICanvasEngine = new CanvasEngine(canvas, model);
function moveObject(counter: number, upperLimit: number) {
    if (counter > upperLimit) {
        return;
    }
    setTimeout(() => {
        shape1.move(new Point(shape1.location.x + 1, shape1.location.y
+ 1));
        engine.invalidate();
        counter++;
        moveObject(counter, upperLimit);
    }, 20);
}
moveObject(0, 75);
```

The preceding code instantiates a `DrawingModel`, adds a shape to it, instantiates `CanvasEngine`, and runs a recursive function that moves the object diagonally across the canvas. The recursive function uses the `setTimeout` function to cause a slight delay in the object's movement, otherwise the object would move faster than we would be able to track it. Again we use the lambda syntax, `() => { }`, but because we are not within an object's constructor, it will only act as a shorthand method for generating a function. However, this application is supposed to be user-focused; so, let's look at how we hook into the mouse events to allow the user to manipulate objects on our canvas.

Mouse events

The first action involved in any interaction between one of our shapes and the mouse will be a selection event. This will be handled by the `mousedown` event associated with the canvas. This will allow us to use the click and hold functionality as well as additional functionality when the mouse is released. The `mousedown` event handler is shown in the following example:

```
private _mousedown(e) {
        var mouse: IPoint = this._getMousePosition(this._canvas, e);
        var i, shape;
        if (this._model.shapes) {
            for (i = this._model.shapes.length - 1; i >= 0; i--) {
                this._model.shapes[i].isSelected = false;
            }
        }
        if (this._model.getDrawingTool() != DrawingToolType.Select) {
            shape = this._model.getNewShape(mouse);
            this._model.addShape(shape);
            this.action = CanvasEngineAction.Resize;
            this._setShapeAsSelected(shape);
            return;
        }
        else if (this._model.shapes) {
            for (i = this._model.shapes.length - 1; i >= 0; i--) {
                this.action = this._model.Shapes[i].
getClickLocationAction(mouse, this.context);
                switch (this.action) {
                    case CanvasEngineAction.Resize:
                    case CanvasEngineAction.Move:
                        var moveOffsetPoint = this._model.shapes[i].
getMoveOffset(mouse);
                        this._dragOffsetX = moveOffsetPoint.X;
                        this._dragOffsetY = moveOffsetPoint.Y;
```

```
                                    this._setShapeAsSelected(this._model.
shapes[i]);

                                    this._bringToFront(i);
                                    return;
                            default:
                                    break;
                    }
                }
            }
            this._clearEngineState();
    }
```

This method starts by getting the point location of the mouse in relation to the canvas. Then, each shape is set to unselected. If the model tells us that the drawing tool is something other than the selection tool, then we will create a new shape, add it to the model, select it, and set the engine's current action to resize so that holding the mouse down will cause the new shape to scale as the mouse moves. So far, we haven't defined any logic to change our drawing tool though, so for now it will always be the selection tool. When the selection tool is active, then we want to loop through the list of shapes in the model and determine whether any action should be taken on them.

 Take note of the fact that we loop backwards through the list this time; however, in the draw method, we proceeded forwards. If we ever have overlapping objects, we want the object shown on top to be the object we operate on.

Once we have requested the action that should be taken on the current shape, we must persist any additional properties that the mousemove or mouseup events could possibly need to complete their actions. This includes determining how far the mouse click is from the drawing shapes current location, setting it as the selected shape, and moving it to the end of the shapes' list; that way, it is rendered last and on top of all other shapes on the canvas. If no action needs to be taken, the engine clears any selections and redraws all of the shapes. The helper methods shown in this method block are shown in the following example:

```
    private _getMousePos(canvas: HTMLCanvasElement, e: MouseEvent):
IPoint {
        var rect = canvas.getBoundingClientRect(),
            root = window.document.documentElement;
        var mouseX = e.clientX - rect.left - root.scrollLeft;
        var mouseY = e.clientY - rect.top - root.scrollTop;
        return new Point(mouseX, mouseY);
    }
    private _setShapeAsSelected(shape: IDrawingShape) {
```

```
        shape.isSelected = true;
        this._model.selection = shape;
        this.invalidate();
    }
    private _clearEngineState() {
        this.action = CanvasEngineAction.None;
        this._model.selection = null;
        this.invalidate();
    }
    private _bringToFront(index: number) {
        var shape = this._model.shapes[index];
        if (shape) {
            this._model.shapes.splice(index, 1);
            this._model.shapes.push(shape);
            this.invalidate();
        }
    }
}
```

Each of these methods performs a very specific function in a very controlled scope. This will come in handy later when we get into unit testing. So at this point, the end user has an object selected on the canvas and wants to manipulate it. These interactions will be handled within the mousemove event. As you can see in the following code sample, manipulating our objects requires very little work from the engine:

```
private _mousemove(e) {
    var mouse: IPoint = this._getMousePosition(this._canvas, e);;
    switch (this.action) {
        case CanvasEngineAction.Move:
            var newLocationX = mouse.x - this._dragOffsetX;
            var newLocationY = mouse.y - this._dragOffsetY;
            var newLocation = new Point(newLocationX, newLocationY);
            this._model.selection.move(newLocation);
            this.invalidate();
            break;
        case CanvasEngineAction.Resize:
            this._model.selection.resizeToLocation(mouse);
            this.invalidate();
            break;
        case CanvasEngineAction.None:
        default:
            var mousePointer = "auto";
            if (this._model.shapes) {
                for (var i = this._model.shapes.length - 1; i >= 0;
    i--) {
```

```
            if (this._model.shapes[i].inResizeZone(mouse) ||
                this._model.shapes[i].contains(mouse, this.
context)) {
                    mousePointer = this._model.shapes[i].
getCursorType(mouse);
                    break;
            }
        }
    }
    window.document.body.style.cursor = mousePointer;
    break;
    }
}
```

This function uses the private state of the engine to determine the action it is supposed to take and call the appropriate method from our IDrawingShape abstraction. This method also accounts for when no shape is selected and the user is moving the mouse around the screen. If no object is selected, the engine determines whether the location of the cursor is available to click for manipulation. We can safely place any concrete implementation of the DrawingShapeBase class through this method and it will be available for interaction with the user. The final piece of this interaction is the mouseup event, which signifies the end of a specific set of user interactions. At this point, the CanvasEngine class will have to reset its state and get ready for another interaction.

```
private _mouseup(e) {
    var selection = this._model.selection;
    if (selection) {
        selection.isSelected = false;
    }
    this._clearEngineState();
}
```

Now, we can run the application and the shapes in our DrawingModel can be moved around the canvas and resized as the user wishes. The next thing we want to do is allow the user to make new shapes because this wouldn't be much of a drawing application if we could only interact with the shapes already on the screen.

User options

We now have a reusable set of shape types, a set of drawing types that contain references to our shapes, an engine to control execution flow, and an object to keep track of and manage the drawing objects. The only thing we are missing is user options to manipulate what action is taken. In this section, we will be modifying our original HTML and finishing the implementation of the DrawingModel type.

The first thing we need to do is add some new buttons. Each one will be associated with a different tool type. As you can see in the following screenshot, we now have three new buttons, each of which displays the name of the tool that it represents:

```html
<!DOCTYPE html>
<html lang="en">
<head>
    <meta charset="utf-8" />
    <title>TypeScript HTML App</title>
    <link rel="stylesheet" href="app.css" type="text/css" />
    <script src="Enums.js"></script>
    <script src="Shapes.js"></script>
    <script src="CanvasEngine.js"></script>
    <script src="DrawingModel.js"></script>
</head>
<body>
    <h1>Drawing Application</h1>
    <div id="content">
        <div>
            <button id="selectButton">Select</button>
            <button id="rectangleButton">Rectangle</button>
            <button id="lineButton">Line</button>
        </div>
        <canvas id="drawingCanvas" height="400" width="570"
                style="border: 4px solid ■black;"/>
    </div>
    <script src="app.js"></script>
</body>
</html>
```

Now that we have the buttons, we need to perform some work when they are clicked. The DrawingModel will handle this work for us since we will need to modify properties of this object directly. We will need to add an event handler for each button that sets a private member of the model to the corresponding drawing tool. In the example of this class earlier, we had an empty constructor; we need to change this so that when the model is created, it starts listening for the click events.

```typescript
private _drawingTool: DrawingToolType = DrawingToolType.Select;
constructor() {
    this._addEventListeners();
}
private _addEventListeners() {
    var selectButton = window.document.
getElementById("selectButton");
    selectButton.addEventListener("click", (e) => {
        this._drawingTool = DrawingToolType.Select;
```

```
            }, true);
            var rectButton = window.document.getElementById("rectangleBut
ton");
            rectButton.addEventListener("click", (e) => {
                this._drawingTool = DrawingToolType.Rectangle;
            }, true);
            var rectButton = window.document.getElementById("lineButton");
            rectButton.addEventListener("click", (e) => {
                this._drawingTool = DrawingToolType.Line;
            }, true);
        }
```

With these event handlers setting the private variable to the appropriate drawing tool, we can now fill in the remainder of this implementation as well. Previously, we left the getNewShape method without a body and the getDrawingTool method always returned the Select tool. Now that we have a private reference to the tool we should be using, getDrawingTool will just return this value. The getNewShape method needs a little more work though. In the following example, you can see that we create the new shape and set some of the initial properties for drawing:

```
    public getNewShape(location: IPoint): IDrawingShape {
        var shape: IDrawingShape = null;
        var cursor: string = "auto";
        switch (this._drawingTool) {
            case DrawingToolType.Rectangle:
                shape = new DrawingRectangle();
                shape.move(location);
                (<DrawingRectangle>shape).shape.height = 3;
                (<DrawingRectangle>shape).shape.width = 3;
                cursor = "se-resize";
                break;
            case DrawingToolType.Line:
                shape = new DrawingLine();
                (<DrawingLine>shape).shape.p1 = location;
                (<DrawingLine>shape).shape.p2 = new Point(location.x +
1, location.y + 1);
                cursor = "e-resize";
                break;
        }
        window.document.body.style.cursor = cursor;
        return shape;
    }
    public getDrawingTool(): DrawingToolType {
        return this._drawingTool;
    }
```

Based on the private state of the model, we either create `DrawingRectangle` or
`DrawingLine`. The full implementation of the `DrawingRectangle` class has been
shown in this text; the implementation of the `DrawingLine` class is available for
download along with all the other code samples in this book. Now we have all of
the components necessary to run our application and allow users to create and
modify shapes as they please. The final code for `app.ts` is as follows:

```
var canvas: HTMLCanvasElement = <HTMLCanvasElement>window.document.get
ElementById("drawingCanvas");
var model: IDrawingModel = new DrawingModel();
var engine: ICanvasEngine = new CanvasEngine(canvas, model);
```

As you can see, the main part of our application does very little work. The canvas
is retrieved from the DOM, `DrawingModel` is instantiated, and finally the engine
is created. When the application is run, all of the event handlers are attached and
everything from that point forward is user-driven.

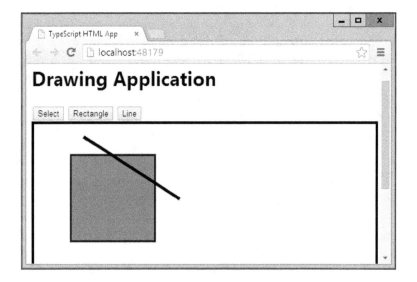

This is a good start, but it would be really nice if we could change the color of the
objects we are drawing. Along with the canvas element, HTML5 includes a color
picker that will launch the browser's color picker dialog and return the six-digit
hex code of the color that was selected. The first thing we need to do is create new
interfaces to support what we want to do. Since the drawing context for the canvas
has both a `fillStyle` and a `strokeStyle` attribute, we might as well adopt a similar
system. These should be separate interfaces because as you can see from the previous
image, a line would have no use for a fill color. So, let's create these two new
interfaces and apply them to our drawing objects:

```
interface IFillStyle {
```

```
    fillStyle: string;
}
interface IStrokeStyle {
    strokeStyle: string;
}
```

Next, we will need to modify the concrete implementations of the drawing objects to implement the appropriate interfaces. We have to modify the DrawingRectangle class to implement the IFillStyle interface and the DrawingLine class to implement the IStrokeStyle interface. In the following screenshot, you can see the modifications made to the DrawingRectangle class:

```
class DrawingRectangle extends DrawingShapeBase implements IFillStyle {
    public shape: IRectangle = new Rectangle(0, 0);
    public fillStyle: string = "#FF0000"
    constructor() [...]
    public inResizeZone(point: IPoint): boolean [...]
    public resizeToLocation(to: IPoint) [...]
    public draw(ctx: CanvasRenderingContext2D) {
        ctx.fillStyle = this.fillStyle;
        ctx.strokeStyle = "#000000";
        ctx.globalAlpha = this.opacity;
        ctx.lineWidth = 3;
        ctx.fillRect(this.location.x, this.location.y, this.shape.width, this.shape.height);
        ctx.strokeRect(this.location.x, this.location.y, this.shape.width, this.shape.height);
    }
    public contains(mousePoint: IPoint, context: CanvasRenderingContext2D): boolean [...]
    public getMoveOffset(mousePosition: IPoint): IPoint [...]
    public getCursorType(mousePoint: IPoint) [...]
}
```

The implements keyword has been added to the class declaration enforcing the type restriction upon DrawingRectangle. The public fillStyle member has been added and initialized. The Draw method only had one minor change which was to set the rendering context's fillStyle to the new fillStyle member. Let's now modify our HTML to include the color picker and give it an ID so that we can add an event handler to it later.

```
<button id="selectButton">Select</button>
<button id="rectangleButton">Rectangle</button>
<button id="lineButton">Line</button>
<input type="color" id="colorPicker" />
```

Now, we can modify the model to change the color of these object types when they are created. First, we must add another event handler to listen for the value of the color picker to change. When this event fires, we will store the value as part of the model's private state and retrieve it during the creation of new shape objects. In the following example, you can see how the model has been modified:

```
    private _drawingColor: string = "#000000";
    private _addEventListeners() {
        var selectButton = window.document.
getElementById("selectButton");
        selectButton.addEventListener("click", (e) => {
            this._drawingTool = DrawingToolType.Select;
        }, true);
        var rectButton = window.document.getElementById("rectangleBut
ton");
        rectButton.addEventListener("click", (e) => {
            this._drawingTool = DrawingToolType.Rectangle;
        }, true);
        var rectButton = window.document.getElementById("lineButton");
        rectButton.addEventListener("click", (e) => {
            this._drawingTool = DrawingToolType.Line;
        }, true);
        var colorPicker = window.document.
getElementById("colorPicker");
        colorPicker.addEventListener("change", (e) => {
            this._drawingColor = (<any>e.currentTarget).value;
        }, true);
    }
    public getNewShape(location: IPoint): IDrawingShape {
        var shape: IDrawingShape = null;
        var cursor: string = "auto";
        switch (this._drawingTool) {
            case DrawingToolType.Rectangle:
                shape = new DrawingRectangle();
                shape.Move(location);
                (<DrawingRectangle>shape).shape.height = 3;
                (<DrawingRectangle>shape).shape.width = 3;
                (<DrawingRectangle>shape).fillStyle = this._
drawingColor;
                cursor = "se-resize";
                break;
            case DrawingToolType.Line:
                shape = new DrawingLine();
```

```
            (<DrawingLine>shape).shape.p1 = location;
            (<DrawingLine>shape).shape.p2 = new Point(location.x +
1, location.y + 1);
            (<DrawingLine>shape).strokeStyle = this._drawingColor;
            cursor = "e-resize";
            break;
    }
    window.document.body.style.cursor = cursor;
    return shape;
}
```

As you can see, we added a new private variable to store the current color value. The extra event handler was added to listen for the color picker's value to change and to store this value. The `getNewShape` code simply sets the appropriate property for the type being instantiated and the shape object handles the rest. As you can see in the following screenshot, we can now create objects of any size or color:

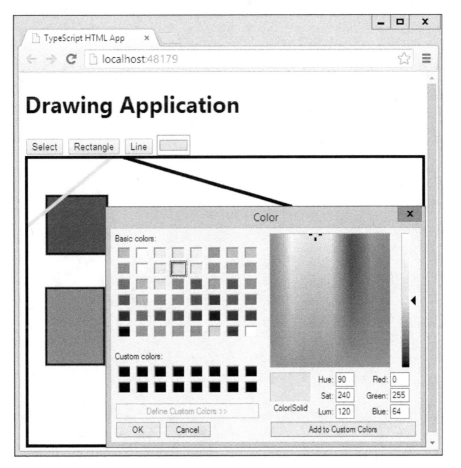

Summary

Throughout this chapter, we have focused on building a drawing application from end to end in TypeScript. We started with the basic building blocks for the application, the abstraction, then created a set of reusable shape objects. These objects are then used in a set of classes responsible for drawing them on an HTML5 canvas. Next, we built an engine responsible for handling user interaction and requesting information from the drawing objects to make decisions. Finally, we built a model to keep track of all of the shape objects in the running application. All of this has been done using TypeScript, and only TypeScript. However, a common practice in web development is integrating with third-party libraries such as jQuery. In the next chapter, we are going to look at some of the available third-party libraries and how to integrate them with your projects.

6
Declaration Files and Library Integrations

So far, we have been writing TypeScript without integrating with any external JavaScript libraries. We have covered the different concepts that the language adds on top of JavaScript and how to use them to our advantage when building large scale applications. We have ignored all of the third-party libraries that are openly available on the Web to improve the JavaScript experience. In this chapter, we will cover declaration files and how they help us integrate with other JavaScript libraries. The topics we are going to cover in this chapter include:

- Declaration files
- The NuGet package manager
- jQuery
- Knockout
- External modules

Declaration files

Declaration files are a special type of source file in TypeScript and have a different file extension. Declaration files have a file extension of .d.ts and they can contain type information but no implementation details. This includes interface definitions as well as type declarations.

Type declarations are created using the `declare` keyword, as shown in the following screenshot:

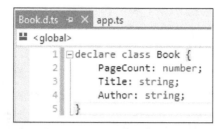

As you can see, the name of the file is `Book.d.ts`, which is how the compiler knows that this file will only contain declarations. When this occurs, no output file is created and an error will be generated when the implementation code is found in the file. The purpose of these files is to provide type information for other JavaScript libraries that are not in TypeScript files. This allows us to interact with these libraries in a strongly typed fashion, providing compile time checks and intelligent code completion. In the previous example, we declare that the `Book` class will exist in the global namespace allowing it to be referenced throughout our project. We can now use `Book` freely, but if an implementation is not provided for it our application will fail during execution wherever the `Book` type is referenced.

As we saw earlier on when looking at the TypeScript compiler and its options, we can automatically generate declaration files for our own code. These declaration files can be referenced from other projects within your own solution or deployed as part of a library you distribute. A declaration file will be output for every JavaScript file that is output. If you combine all of your code into a single file then a single declaration file will be created. Selecting the **Generate declaration files** option from the TypeScript build section of the project properties will provide the compiler with the appropriate parameter used to create our declaration files, as shown in the following screenshot:

Output
- ☐ Keep comments in JavaScript output
- ☐ Combine JavaScript output into file:
- ☐ Redirect JavaScript output to directory:
- ☑ Generate declaration files

Throughout this book, we have used a variety of types that weren't explicitly declared by us. The `CanvasRenderingContext2D` object we used in our drawing application had a full list of type information in Visual Studio IntelliSense, yet we never saw its declaration or implementation. This is because TypeScript comes with a `lib.d.ts` file that declares type information for thousands of different objects. This declaration file is automatically referenced every time the compiler runs. This list of types is incredibly useful but it doesn't include any types from external libraries that may or may not be referenced in your projects.

Third-party library integration

One of the key components in large scale web development is the use of open source libraries that handle certain tasks for us. jQuery is one of the more popular libraries and is used for easy interaction with the **Document Object Model (DOM)**. These libraries provide a wide variety of functionalities but all of these interactions can be given some level of typing. In this section, we are going to look at the following libraries:

- jQuery
- Knockout
- RequireJS

Before we start developing these libraries, we need to get them referenced in our project. Each of these libraries can be downloaded directly from their web pages or through the use of NuGet. NuGet is a package manager for Visual Studio and can be installed as an extension.

Installing NuGet packages

The first thing we need to do is install the NuGet Package Manager. To do this, first select **Tools** from the menu and choose **Extensions and Updates**. This will bring you to a screen showing all of the extensions you currently have installed as well as provide you with the ability to find more online.

Select the **Online** section in the tree view on the left and search for **NuGet Package Manager**, as shown in the following screenshot:

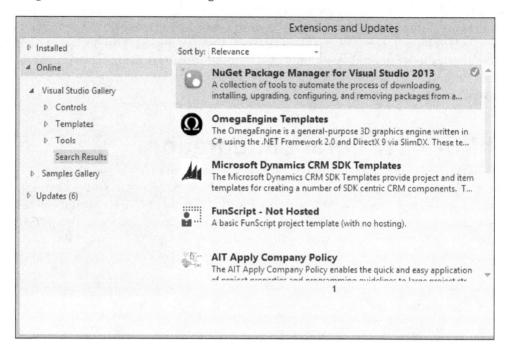

Once you locate the package manager, download and install it. After this process is complete, Visual Studio will need to be restarted before we can start consuming packages.

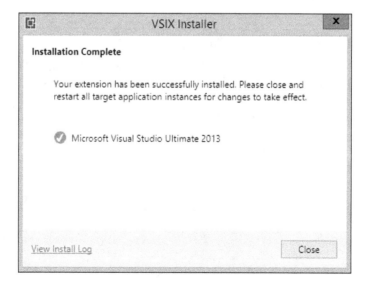

The NuGet packages we will be installing will include the code for the libraries we will be using as well as separate declaration files for each of these libraries. Not every library has NuGet packages or declaration files associated with them, however, the web development community is very good about filling in these holes. There is a large repository of TypeScript library declaration files available from the **DefinitelyTyped** repository on GitHub.

Integrating with jQuery

jQuery is one of the most popular open source libraries available on the Web. It can be used for anything from DOM manipulation to simplifying remote server calls. If you plan on building a large scale web application you were probably already planning on using jQuery and if not, I strongly recommend that you do. To start using jQuery, the first thing we need to do is install the jQuery NuGet package. Right-click on the project and select **Manage NuGet Packages**. This will bring up a window similar to the updates and extensions window. Locate jQuery from the nuget.org repository in the **Online** section and install it. As you can see in the following screenshot, several files are installed with this package that help us develop with jQuery:

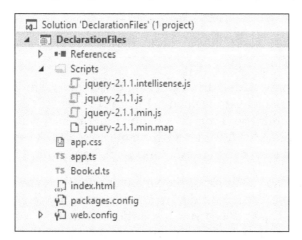

Now we can add a script tag the `index.html` file and jQuery will be available at runtime for us to use. This, however, isn't very useful during development and compilation of our TypeScript code because we don't have any type information about the library. To import this type information, we need a declaration file that represents the jQuery library. Open up the **Manage NuGet Packages** window again and search for `jQuery.TypeScript`. Install the package named **jquery.TypeScript. DefinitelyTyped**, which is on Version 1.3.5 at the time of writing this, to import the type information of the jQuery library.

> There are a number of other libraries that extend jQuery and quite a few declaration files have been created to support these different extensions.

Now that the type information for jQuery has been included in the project we will be able to use the library in a more robust way. Let's add some elements to our HTML that we will manipulate with the jQuery library.

```
index.html  ×  app.ts
 1  <!DOCTYPE html>
 2  <html lang="en">
 3  <head>
 4      <meta charset="utf-8" />
 5      <title>TypeScript HTML App</title>
 6      <link rel="stylesheet" href="app.css" type="text/css" />
 7      <script src="Scripts/jquery-2.1.1.js" ></script>
 8      <script src="app.js"></script>
 9  </head>
10  <body>
11      <h1>TypeScript HTML App</h1>
12
13      <div id="content">
14          <div id="colorPanel" style="background-color: ■blue; height: 300px; width: 300px;">
15          </div>
16          <button id="hideButton" >Hide</button>
17      </div>
18  </body>
19  </html>
```

As you can see, we have added the `script` tag for jQuery to the document's `head` tag, and a couple of elements to the body. The first element is a large square `div` with a blue background. The second is a button that the user will click to hide the blue `div` tag that is shown. Now that we have the objects we want to manipulate, let's create some TypeScript to perform the expected operation.

In order to use jQuery in a strongly typed manner with the TypeScript compiler, we must include a reference to the declaration file at the top of the TypeScript file we wish to use it in. This is done using a specific format at the top of the TypeScript file; placing references anywhere but at the top of the page will cause them not to function. In the following example, you can see how to reference declaration files:

```
/// <reference path="scripts/typings/jquery/jquery.d.ts" />
```

The path included in the reference is relative to the file you are currently working in. Once this reference has been added, we are able to use IntelliSense and code completion to help us work with the jQuery API.

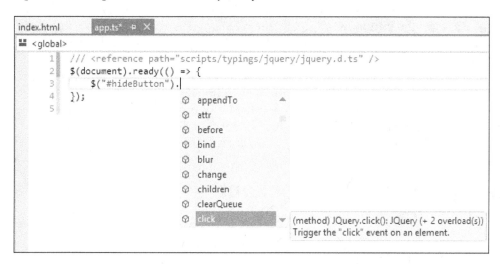

As you can see, we get the full feature set associated with Visual Studio's code completion.

When integrating with a large number of libraries it can be easier to manage your references by creating a _references.d.ts file and added references only to this file. Then, each of your code files only has to reference the single _references.d.ts file to import all of the relevant type information for the project.

As you can see in the following code sample, locating objects on the DOM and manipulating them is far easier with jQuery included and will reduce the amount of code we have to produce to make a dynamic application:

```
/// <reference path="scripts/typings/jquery/jquery.d.ts" />
$(document).ready(() => {
    $("#hideButton").click((event) => {
        $("#colorPanel").hide(1000);
    });
});
```

The first element in the file is the reference to the jQuery declaration file. This is what allows us to use the $ notation in our TypeScript without generating a compiler error, however, jQuery still needs to be loaded for this to work at runtime. We wait for the DOM to finish loading, which causes the function delegate to be called. At this time, we select the button we added to our HTML earlier on and listen for its click event to fire. When this occurs, another function delegate is called, which uses one of jQuery's UI modification methods called hide to make the large square div tag disappear over a period of 1000 milliseconds. Now if the application is run, there will be a large blue square just above the hide button. Once the button is clicked, you can watch the blue box disappear and the UI adjust for its disappearance. jQuery has a very large set of features and extensions. To learn more about this I recommend visiting http://jquery.com/ for an API reference and samples.

Integrating with Knockout

Software development in thick client applications, applications installed on the desktop, using technologies such as WPF have adopted new patterns to interact with the UI. Primary among these is the Model-View-ViewModel pattern, which aims to separate our business logic from the client application logic. Knockout is a JavaScript library that is meant to facilitate this pattern in the browser. You can install Knockout through the NuGet Package Manager as well as the declaration file for use in TypeScript. The packages used for this text are knockoutjs Version 3.1.0 and knockout.TypeScript.DefinitelyTyped Version 0.5.4. Knockout is dependent upon jQuery being available so make sure it is part of the project as well.

Knockout creates objects known as observables that other objects can subscribe to and will be notified if the value changes. When a value changes, the watchers can optionally take action on the new value of the observable. This comes in very handy when combined with Knockout's binding engine that allows us to bind our TypeScript/JavaScript objects to DOM elements. Let's take a look at an example of this binding. The first thing we need to do is create a ViewModel. This will be a class that contains observables and methods that we can bind to in the HTML of the application:

```
/// <reference path="scripts/typings/jquery/jquery.d.ts" />
/// <reference path="scripts/typings/knockout/knockout.d.ts" />
class ViewModel {
    public toggleText: KnockoutObservable<string> =
ko.observable("Hide");
    public isVisible: KnockoutObservable<boolean> =
ko.observable(true);
    constructor() {
    }
```

```
    public toggleClick(viewModel: ViewModel, event: JQueryEventObject)
{
        if (this.isVisible()) {
            this.toggleText("Show");
            this.isVisible(false);
        } else {
            this.toggleText("Hide");
            this.isVisible(true);
        }
    }
}
```

As you can see, we create two observable objects providing the specific type as a type parameter using the generic syntax we discussed in *Chapter 2, TypeScript Basics*. The toggleText observable contains a string value that will be displayed on a button in our UI. The second observable holds a Boolean value that will determine whether an object in the DOM is visible to the user or not. Finally, we have a method that will be bound to a button click event and will change the value of these observables. This object will be bound to our HTML using the data-bind syntax defined by the Knockout API. The HTML code in the following screenshot shows our bindings:

```
index.html  ╤ ✕  app.ts
 1    <!DOCTYPE html>
 2  ⊟<html lang="en">
 3  ⊟<head>
 4        <meta charset="utf-8" />
 5        <title>TypeScript HTML App</title>
 6        <link rel="stylesheet" href="app.css" type="text/css" />
 7        <script src="Scripts/jquery-2.1.1.js" ></script>
 8        <script src="Scripts/knockout-3.1.0.js"></script>
 9        <script src="app.js"></script>
10    </head>
11  ⊟<body>
12        <h1>TypeScript HTML App</h1>
13
14  ⊟    <div id="content">
15  ⊟        <div id="colorPanel" data-bind="visible: isVisible"
16              style="background-color: ■blue; height: 300px; width: 300px;">
17            </div>
18            <button id="toggleButton"
19                data-bind="text: toggleText, click: toggleClick" ></button>
20        </div>
21    </body>
22    </html>
23    |
```

As you can see, we include the jQuery and Knockout libraries in `head`. Then, in the body of the HTML, we have the two elements we created during the jQuery example. However, each of these elements now contains bindings. The `colorPanel` div is bound to the `IsVisible` observable using Knockout's visible binding. When the `IsVisible` observable changes, Knockout will evaluate the new value and manipulate the DOM to show or hide the div. The button is bound to multiple elements on the view model, the `toggleText` object, which will determine what the value of the button is, and the `toggleClick` method, which will execute anytime the click event fires.

 Knockout supports many different kinds of bindings and also has a custom binding model that will allow you to define your own bindings. Visit www.knockoutjs.com to learn more.

OK, we have most of the pieces together now to dynamically bind the DOM to our TypeScript/JavaScript but we need to actually connect the view and the view model. The following code segment shows how to bind the two together:

```
$(document).ready(() => {
    ko.applyBindings(new ViewModel());
});
```

As you can see, we wait for the DOM to be ready before we apply the binding. If we attempt to bind before all of the elements are available an error will occur at runtime. Once the DOM is ready, we create a new instance of our `ViewModel` class and pass it to Knockout, which will handle the rest. Optionally, you can pass in a specific element to bind the view model to. Now when we run the application it starts with the large blue square visible and the text of the button is **Hide**. However, instead of this being the end of the application's life cycle as it was earlier, the button text has changed and we can perform another action, as shown in the following screenshot:

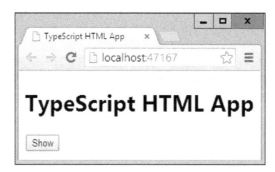

Using RequireJS

In *Chapter 2, TypeScript Basics*, we discussed module definitions but at the time we only focused on internal modules. At the time, external modules were mentioned but we did not explore them in-depth. Now that we are familiar with integrating external libraries we will bring in one of the more common external module libraries available. RequireJS is a JavaScript module loader used to ensure that all objects being used during application execution are available when necessary. This will allow us to separate our code into different files and not worry about the order in which they are loaded because RequireJS will manage that for us. Just like jQuery and Knockout, RequireJS and its declaration file are available through the NuGet Package Manager or can be found online at `www.requirejs.org`. The packages used for this text are "RequireJS" Version 2.1.14 and `requires.TypeScript.DefinitelyTyped` Version 0.2.0. For this next example, we will need all three libraries available. Let's put together a simple app that will allow us to add people to a directory and then search that directory.

RequireJS is an **Asynchronous Module Loader (AMD)** so we need to set the appropriate project settings. Open the TypeScript Build section of the project settings and set the Module system option to AMD. Now, we need to create a new module that will contain all of the code related to a set of types that represent people for the directory. Create a new TypeScript file called `People.ts` in the `Scripts` folder of the project. As you can see in the following sample, we define the `IPerson` abstraction and then implement it:

```
export interface IPerson {
    firstName: string;
    lastName: string;
    age: number;
}
export class Person implements IPerson {
    constructor(public firstName: string, public lastName: string,
public age: number) {
    }
}
```

Both the `IPerson` interface and `Person` class are decorated with the `export` keyword, which will tell the compiler that these types are available in other modules that use this module. The resulting JavaScript is a little different from what was generated for internal modules:

```
define(["require", "exports"], function(require, exports) {
    (function (People) {
```

```
        var Person = (function () {
            function Person(firstName, lastName, age) {
                this.firstName = firstName;
                this.lastName = lastName;
                this.age = age;
            }
            return Person;
        })();
        People.Person = Person;
    })(exports.People || (exports.People = {}));
    var People = exports.People;
});
```

As you can see, the normal module definition is wrapped in another function called define that takes an array of dependent objects and a function to be called when all of the dependent modules are loaded. The next thing we need to create is a view model that we can bind our HTML to. We will need observables for the three input values for new people, the value that we want to search against, and an observable array to hold the search results. We will also need a method to initiate the addition process and a method to perform a directory search. We can place all of this code in a separate TypeScript file and use the import and require keywords to include the People module we just created:

```
import People = require("Scripts/People");
export class PersonFinderViewModel {
    public peopleArray: KnockoutObservableArray<People.IPerson> =
ko.observableArray([]);
    public newFirstName: KnockoutObservable<string> =
ko.observable("");
    public newLastName: KnockoutObservable<string> =
ko.observable("");
    public newAge: KnockoutObservable<number> = ko.observable(null);
    public searchValue: KnockoutObservable<string> =
ko.observable("");
    public searchResult: KnockoutObservableArray<People.IPerson> =
ko.observableArray([]);
    constructor() {
    }
    public findPersonByFirstName(viewModel: PersonFinderViewModel,
event: JQueryEventObject) {
        var people = this.peopleArray();
```

```
        var searchValue = this.searchValue();
        this.searchResult([]);
        for (var i = 0; i < people.length; i++) {
            if (searchValue === people[i].firstName) {
                this.searchResult.push(people[i]);
            }
        }
    }
    public addNewPerson(viewModel: PersonFinderViewModel, event:
JQueryEventObject) {
        var newPerson = new People.Person(this.newFirstName(), this.
newLastName(), this.newAge());
        this.peopleArray.push(newPerson);
        this.newFirstName("");
        this.newLastName("");
        this.newAge(null);
    }
}
```

As you can see, we provide the path to the People module to the require function, which tells RequireJS to add the module to the list of modules given to the define method, but also the TypeScript compiler for type information. We define a list of people that will be stored as the full directory list, the new people field observables, the search observables, and the two methods that will be bound to click events. The findPersonByFirstName method retrieves the most recent value of the searchValue observable as well as the list of people that we will be searching against.

If you are going to reference an observable or observable collection several times during a single execution block, it is faster to retrieve the value of the observable a single time, as shown in the findPersonByFirstName method. However, any modifications to the values should be made directly against the observables.

The existing set of search results is cleared to make way for new results. Finally, we iterate through the list of people and compare the search value to the first name of the current person. If there is a match, we add it to the list and continue on. The addNewPerson method retrieves all of the current values for the new person input values and passes them to the constructor of the Person class inside the People module. This person is then added to the observable array and the fields are cleared for a new entry.

Now that we have domain objects and a view model, we need to create the HTML to represent our application. Normally, we would have to add script tags for all of our JavaScript source files but since we are now using `require` we only need to add a few.

```html
index.html
1    <!DOCTYPE html>
2    <html lang="en">
3    <head>
4        <meta charset="utf-8" />
5        <title>TypeScript HTML App</title>
6        <link rel="stylesheet" href="app.css" type="text/css" />
7        <script src="Scripts/jquery-2.1.1.js"></script>
8        <script src="Scripts/knockout-3.1.0.debug.js"></script>
9        <script data-main="app.js" src="Scripts/require.js"></script>
10   </head>
11   <body>
12       <h1>TypeScript HTML App</h1>
13       <div id="content">
14           <div>
15               <div>
16                   <div>
17                       <label>First Name: </label>
18                       <input type="text" data-bind="value: newFirstName" />
19                   </div>
20                   <div>
21                       <label>Last Name: </label>
22                       <input type="text" data-bind="value: newLastName" />
23                   </div>
24                   <div>
25                       <label>Age: </label>
26                       <input type="number" data-bind="value: newAge" />
27                   </div>
28               </div>
29               <button data-bind="click: addNewPerson">Add New</button>
30           </div>
31           <input type="text" data-bind="value: searchValue" />
32           <button data-bind="click: findPersonByFirstName">Search</button>
33           <div data-bind="foreach: searchResult" >
34               <div>
35                   <label data-bind="text: firstName"></label>
36                   <label data-bind="text: lastName"></label>
37                   <label data-bind="text: age"></label>
38               </div>
39           </div>
40       </div>
41   </body>
42   </html>
43
```

We include the references to jQuery and Knockout that will sit on the global namespace and then we have a script tag for `require`. Included in the tag for `require` is a binding called `data-main` that is used to define the entry point for the application.

 For more information regarding RequireJS please visit http://requirejs.org/.

In the body of the HTML, we have labels and inputs defining our UI and binding to each of the different objects in our view model. The search results section is doing something new that is worth noting. Using the `foreach` binding on the `searchResult` observable array, we have created a template for every item in the array. The context for these bindings is based on the type of the item being iterated over, in our case a `Person` object. While the `firstName`, `lastName`, and `Age` properties are not observables that can be bound to, the binding will only occur once. If the value of these fields change, the UI will not be updated. The last thing we need to do is create the entry point of our application. We will need to import the view model we created, wait for the DOM to be ready, and apply our bindings:

```
import PersonFinderViewModel = require("Scripts/
PersonFinderViewModel");
$(document).ready(() => {
    ko.applyBindings(new PersonFinderViewModel.
PersonFinderViewModel());
});
```

Now we can run the application and add several users to the directory. When we perform a search for someone by their first name, all of the matching results will be displayed:

Summary

In this chapter, we looked at declaration files and how to generate our own. We installed the NuGet extension for Visual Studio, allowing us to easily install third-party libraries for applications. Then, we covered some of the more common web application libraries in jQuery and Knockout that can be used to easily create large, dynamic, and interactive applications. Finally, we covered external modules and RequireJS to optimize the loading of our modules. In the next chapter, we will use these new tools to improve both our code and the user experience of the drawing application created in *Chapter 5, Creating a Simple Drawing Application*.

7
Enhancing the Drawing Application

When we started the drawing application in *Chapter 5, Creating a Simple Drawing Application*, we grouped all of our code together by functionality. This allowed us to reduce the number of script tags required for our application to work. Using what we learned in the previous chapter, we will modify the drawing application to use AMD modules and RequireJS. We will also integrate Knockout and jQuery to improve the overall user experience. Finally, we will look at how we can use RequireJS to build all of our application code into a single minified file for deployment optimization. The enhancements we will make to our application include:

- Converting to AMD modules
- Binding user controls
- Generating a single output file
- Styling the application

Converting to AMD modules

Converting to AMD modules is a fairly simple process. However, this is a good time to look at the structure and maintainability of our project. Before getting started, we must install the **RequireJS** NuGet package Version 2.1.14 and the corresponding declaration file **requirejs.TypeScript.DefinitelyTyped** Version 0.2.0.

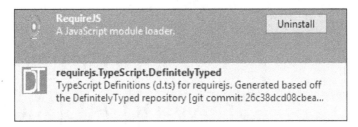

The TypeScript build settings must also be changed to use the AMD module system as shown in the previous chapter. Once these steps are completed, we can begin enhancing our application. To do this, we will want to add a folder structure to our application that will help us easily separate modules based on functionality. At this point, it is important to decide how you want to divide up the code for your application. Since we are using RequireJS modules, we will be using the export keyword for all objects that we want to use from other modules. There are three ways to use the export keyword, and each one has different ramifications on the resulting JavaScript. The following example shows the more common use of the keyword:

```
export class Freehand implements IFreehand {
    public points: Array<IPoint> = [];
    constructor() {
    }
    public AddPoint(point: IPoint) {
        this.points.push(point);
    }
}
```

In this example, the export keyword annotates the type declaration. This tells the TypeScript compiler to place this type on the exports object of the module being generated.

The export keyword is only available when the -- module flag is provided to the compiler. An attempt to use it without providing this option will result in a compiler error. Visual Studio provides this flag when you select a module system in the TypeScript Build section of the project properties.

The resulting JavaScript from this class definition will look very similar to our previous module definitions. However, there will be some special syntax added since we have chosen to use AMD modules:

```
define(["require", "exports"], function(require, exports) {
    var Freehand = (function () {
        function Freehand() {
            this.points = [];
        }
        Freehand.prototype.AddPoint = function (point) {
            this.points.push(point);
        };
        return Freehand;
    })();
    exports.Freehand = Freehand;
});
```

The differences between an AMD module and a standard JavaScript module are apparent from the very beginning of the definition. The AMD specification provides a function called define that is used to assist the module loader. While there are only two parameters shown for this function here, the function optionally takes a third parameter that precedes the two shown in the generated JavaScript code. This optional first parameter is an identifier for the module, and we will look at this parameter in more detail later in this chapter when we want to minify our final application code. The second parameter for the define function is a list of module dependencies. Every require statement that we use to reference another module in our project will be included in this list. The third and final parameter is the only mandatory parameter for us to define a module, and it is a function that will execute to instantiate an object or module. Each of the dependencies provided to the define function will be provided as parameters to the function for use inside of the module.

The export keyword can also be assigned to a type. In the following example, you can see that rather than decorating our class with the export keyword, we instead use the assignment operator to give it a new value:

```
class Circle implements ICircle {
    constructor(public radius: number) {
    }
    public resize(radius: number) {
        this.radius = radius;
    }
    public area(): number {
        return Math.PI * this.radius * this.radius;
    }
}
export = Circle;
```

Using this method limits us to exporting a single type from a file; however, this type can be a module containing any number of exported objects. The resulting JavaScript looks like the following code:

```
define(["require", "exports"], function(require, exports) {
    var Circle = (function () {
        function Circle(radius) {
            this.radius = radius;
        }
        Circle.prototype.resize = function (radius) {
            this.radius = radius;
        };
        Circle.prototype.area = function () {
            return Math.PI * this.radius * this.radius;
        };
        return Circle;
    })();

    return Circle;
});
```

As you can see, the object being exported is no longer placed on the exports object, but is instead the `return` value of the function used by the module loader. Both of these uses are completely valid, but they have a significant effect on how we use the types that we have defined. When decorating the type definition with the `export` keyword, any other segment of code attempting to use that type must require the module and then access it through the module name, as shown in the following screenshot:

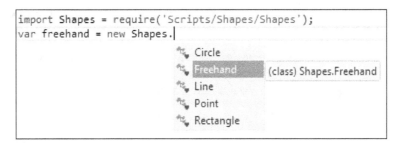

In this example, the path used to reference modules is built relative to the project directory. The RequireJS API allows you to change this path using a configuration file. For more information about the RequireJS API and configuration files, please visit `http://requirejs.org/docs/api.html`.

However, when we use the assignment method to export a type, we have direct access to that object when we import it into another code block, as you can see in the following screenshot:

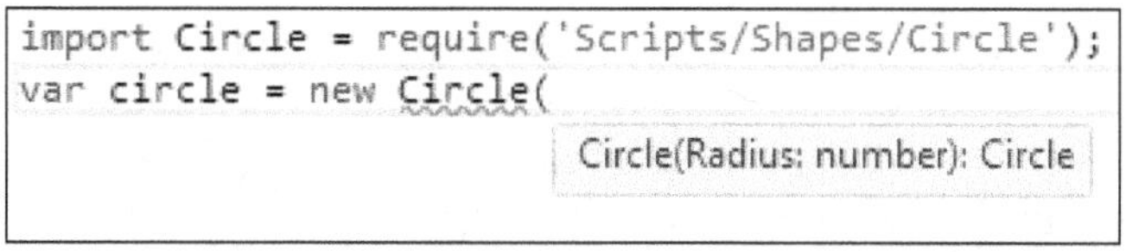

```
import Circle = require('Scripts/Shapes/Circle');
var circle = new Circle(
                            Circle(Radius: number): Circle
```

The third and final use of the export keyword is to attach an imported type to the exports object. When this is done, the imported object isn't just available through its own definition, but we will also be able to access it through the module that exports it. The following sample shows how this is done:

```
export import CanvasEngineAction = require('Scripts/Drawing/Enums/
CanvasEngineAction');
export import DrawingToolType = require('Scripts/Drawing/Enums/
DrawingToolType');
```

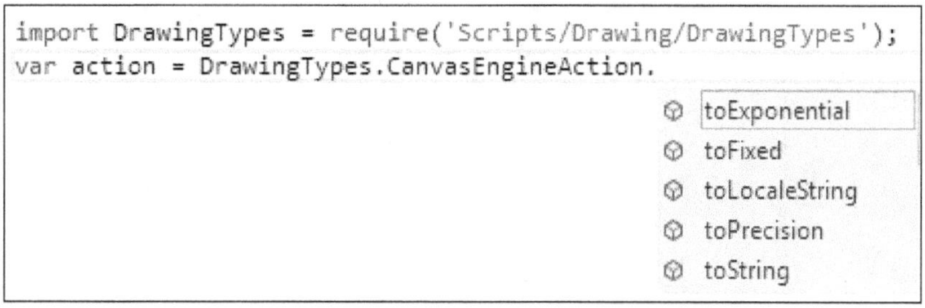

```
import DrawingTypes = require('Scripts/Drawing/DrawingTypes');
var action = DrawingTypes.CanvasEngineAction.
                                          ⊕  toExponential
                                          ⊕  toFixed
                                          ⊕  toLocaleString
                                          ⊕  toPrecision
                                          ⊕  toString
```

Hang on a minute; those aren't the values for our enumeration. What went wrong? Well, this has something to do with the way that the compiler interprets the return type of the CanvasEngineAction enum that was imported and then exported. Enumerations are a clever representation of a number, so the type system reads the return type as a number and determines that these must be our available options. Modules and classes do not have this problem because their type is unique. To work around this problem, we simply have to correctly type the action variable and our enumeration will behave as expected.

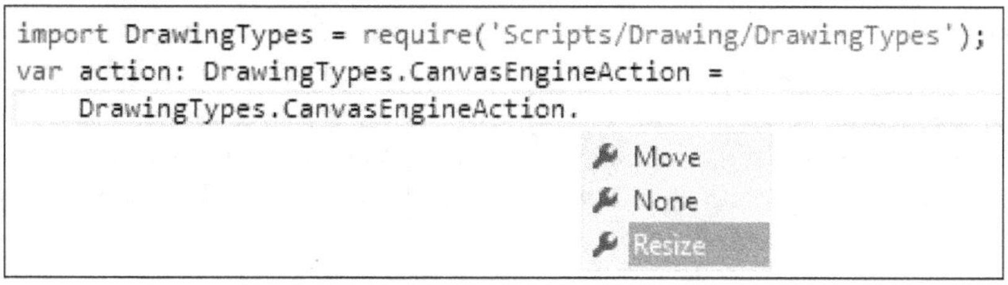

```
import DrawingTypes = require('Scripts/Drawing/DrawingTypes');
var action: DrawingTypes.CanvasEngineAction =
    DrawingTypes.CanvasEngineAction.
                                  🔧  Move
                                  🔧  None
                                  🔧  Resize
```

All of these methods are completely valid and fit different needs. As we refactor the drawing application, we will use a combination of these methods to break our code into logical groupings. Using the TypeScript compiler isn't the only way for us to segment out our code. Keeping code in a directory structure that groups similar objects together results in easy differentiation between code functionality. In the following screenshot, you can see that we have created a separate directory for our generic shape objects from any drawing-related logic. The drawing code is separated into more finely-grained subsections as well depending on the functionality each grouping will contain.

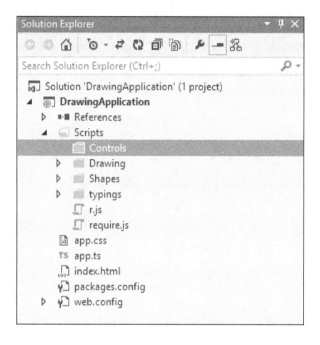

Now we can start breaking our code into separate files, each serving a different and specific purpose. All of our interface types for a specific area can be placed into a single TypeScript file called <Area>Types.ts, for example, `ShapeTypes.ts`. This will give us a place to reference interfaces and enumerations while keeping our classes and actual implementation code separate. Each interface should be decorated with the `export` keyword to ensure that we are able to interact with all of these types in a consistent manner. Next, we need to decide how to structure our implementation code. Each of the different shape objects could be broken into a separate code file and placed inside the `Shapes` directory that we created. However, the amount of code in these classes is minimal and relatively easy to manage, so we can easily place them all inside of a single module. If the implementations start to grow in size like with the drawing-related objects, we will want separate files for each type to keep the code clear and easy to maintain.

The complete contents of the `Shapes.ts` file is shown in the following code:

```
import ShapeTypes = require('Scripts/Shapes/ShapeTypes');
export class Point implements ShapeTypes.IPoint {
    constructor(public X: number, public Y: number) {
    }
}
export class Line implements ShapeTypes.ILine {
    constructor(public p1: ShapeTypes.IPoint, public p2: ShapeTypes.
IPoint) {
    }
    public Length(): number {
        var a2 = Math.pow(this.p2.X - this.p1.X, 2);
        var b2 = Math.pow(this.p2.Y - this.p1.Y, 2);
        return Math.sqrt(a2 + b2);
    }
}
export class Rectangle implements ShapeTypes.IRectangle {
    constructor(public Height: number, public Width: number) {
    }
    public Resize(height: number, width: number) {
        this.Height = height;
        this.Width = width;
    }
}
export class Freehand implements ShapeTypes.IFreehand {
    public Points: Array<ShapeTypes.IPoint> = [];
    constructor() {
    }
    public AddPoint(point: ShapeTypes.IPoint) {
        this.Points.push(point);
    }
}
export class Circle implements ShapeTypes.ICircle {
    constructor(public Radius: number) {
    }
    public Resize(radius: number) {
        this.Radius = radius;
    }
    public Area(): number {
        return Math.PI * this.Radius * this.Radius;
    }
}
```

As you can see, we import the ShapeTypes module, which gives us access to all of the abstractions we created for the shapes. Normally, interfaces are available at the global level in the TypeScript type system. However, because we decorated them with the export keyword, they have been placed on a module type that has no associated code. We reference each of the interfaces through this module type. However, the resulting JavaScript contains no reference to it. Now, we should move into the **Drawing** area of the application and divide up those types accordingly. We will start with the interfaces and enumerations because they are the most basic types and the implementation code won't work without them.

Each enumeration can be placed in its own file, while all of the interfaces will be placed in a single DrawingTypes.ts file. Since some of our interfaces reference the enumerations, we will need to import them into the DrawingTypes file. This is a particularly good time to use the export and import keywords in conjunction to attach the enumerations to the DrawingTypes module. This will allow us to access each of these enumerations in the same way that we access the interfaces in our application. Next, let's break up the drawing shapes into separate files. Each one of these classes requires a significant amount of code, and having them separated into individual code files will make it easier for us to maintain them. The following screenshot shows each of the different files in the Drawing directory:

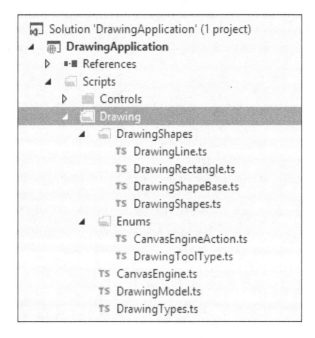

We will recombine them into a single module called `DrawingShapes` that we will use to directly access these types. The `DrawingShapes` module is nothing more than a list of `export` imports, as shown in the following code:

```
export import DrawingShapeBase = require('Scripts/Drawing/
DrawingShapes/DrawingShapeBase');
export import DrawingRectangle = require('Scripts/Drawing/
DrawingShapes/DrawingRectangle');
export import DrawingLine = require('Scripts/Drawing/DrawingShapes/
DrawingLine');
```

The `DrawingModel` and `CanvasEngine` files will import the modules they need and assign the classes they contain to the `export` object. With all of our code now in AMD modules, we can modify our HTML to load only the main entry point to our application, `app.js`, which resides in the root directory of the project, and the rest of the modules will be loaded as necessary through program execution.

```html
index.html

 1    <!DOCTYPE html>
 2    <html lang="en">
 3    <head>
 4        <meta charset="utf-8" />
 5        <title>TypeScript HTML App</title>
 6        <link rel="stylesheet" href="app.css" type="text/css" />
 7    </head>
 8    <body>
 9        <h1>Drawing Application</h1>
10        <div id="content">
11            <div>
12                <button id="selectButton">Select</button>
13                <button id="rectangleButton">Rectangle</button>
14                <button id="lineButton">Line</button>
15                <input type="color" id="colorPicker" />
16            </div>
17            <canvas id="drawingCanvas" height="400" width="570"
18                    style="border: 4px solid ■black;"/>
19        </div>
20        <script data-main="app.js" src="Scripts/require.js"></script>
21    </body>
22    </html>
```

Binding the user controls

Now that we have converted our application to use AMD modules, let's gradually increase the complexity of the application. Currently, we search the DOM for individual elements and attach event handlers to them. This isn't necessarily a bad thing; however, it does leave our code vulnerable to a number of possible issues. The DOM may not have finished rendering the objects we are attempting to attach to, or the object could have been removed by another segment of code. Another pitfall of this approach is that if we wanted to add another drawing shape type to our application, we would have to add another element to the HTML and then more code to add the event handler. This is inefficient and could open up the possibility of making a mistake somewhere. Fortunately, there are a number of libraries available that allow us to implement binding patterns such as **Model View Controller (MVC)** and **Model View ViewModel (MVVM)**. Knockout is one of these libraries, and it brings MVVM to JavaScript and TypeScript development.

Reusable controls

In the previous chapter, we learned about Knockout and its `foreach` binding that allows us to create a template in HTML that each object in an array will be bound to. We will apply the same concept to each of the options we have for our drawing application. Some of these objects are very similar in type and functionality, such as the type selection controls. However, the color picker has a very different interface to implement. This is where the Knockout template binding will come in handy.

The Knockout template binding allows us to provide an HTML template for a specific object type. This gives us the ability to create a separation between our HTML and the JavaScript that is running. In this case, we will have a list of user controls that will be displayed in the space above our canvas object. Before we create the template that we want to bind to, we will need to define the abstraction they will be bound to. The top layer of this abstraction will be the `IUserControl` type, which will contain two properties, `id` and `templateName`, and will be the minimum requirement for binding our DOM elements to:

```
export interface IUserControl {
    id: string;
    templateName: string;
}
```

We will also need interfaces to represent the tool selection buttons and the color picker. These interfaces are more specific to their direct functionality, but as long as they provide a template name that matches it, all of our bindings will flow seamlessly. These interfaces will be defined in a file called `ControlsTypes.ts` in the `Controls` directory and can be seen in the following code:

```
export interface IUpdateObservable {
    observable: KnockoutObservable<any>;
}
export interface IToolSelectionControl extends IUserControl,
IUpdateObservable {
    toolType: DrawingTypes.DrawingToolType;
    click(viewModel: any, event: JQueryEventObject);
    observable: KnockoutObservable<DrawingTypes.DrawingToolType>;
    buttonText: KnockoutObservable<string>;
}
export interface IColorSelectionControl extends IUserControl,
IUpdateObservable {
    change(viewModel: any, event: JQueryEventObject);
    observable: KnockoutObservable<string>;
}
```

As you can see, the `IToolSelectionControl` interface has a `toolType` property that will store the value that this control will be responsible for. There is also a `click` function that will serve as an event handler in the HTML bindings we will create shortly. The remaining two objects are Knockout observables, one of which will be used to inform the calling application that a new tool has been selected and the other will define the text that is displayed by the button. The `IColorSelectionControl` interface extends `IUserControl` in the same way that the `IToolSelectionControl` interface does, but the additional properties here are very different. This interface defines a `change` method that will be called when the color input change event fires. The final property of this interface is very similar to the `observable` property on the `IToolSelectionControl` interface. The primary difference between the two is that they store different types; in this case, we store the string value that represents the current color. Due to the close relationship between these two interfaces, we abstracted the `IUpdateObservable` interface out and then provided a more specific type definition experience within the more finely-grained interfaces.

Now that we have our interfaces defined, we can build our HTML templates to represent the different controls we wish to create. The first template will contain only a button element that has bindings of its own applied to it. The second template is the color picker with a different set of bindings that is unique to this element type. The final thing we must do is modify the area of our HTML that currently holds our controls. As you can see, the resulting HTML has no direct controls defined, but as controls are added to an observable list called `userControls`, they will appear in our application:

```html
index.html
1    <!DOCTYPE html>
2    <html lang="en">
3    <head>
4        <meta charset="utf-8" />
5        <title>TypeScript HTML App</title>
6        <link rel="stylesheet" href="app.css" type="text/css" />
7        <link rel="stylesheet" href="DrawingApplication.css" type="text/css" />
8        <script src="Scripts/jquery-2.1.1.js" ></script>
9        <script src="Scripts/knockout-3.1.0.js"></script>
10       <script data-main="app" src="Scripts/require.js"></script>
11   </head>
12   <body>
13       <h1>Drawing Application</h1>
14       <div id="content">
15           <div data-bind="foreach: userControls">
16               <span data-bind="attr: { id: id }, template: { name: templateName }"></span>
17           </div>
18           <canvas id="drawingCanvas" height="400" width="570" />
19       </div>
20   </body>
21   </html>
22   <script type="text/html" id="ButtonTemplate">
23       <button class="tool-select-button" data-bind="text: buttonText, click: click,
24               css: { 'selected': isSelected }" />
25   </script>
26   <script type="text/html" id="ColorPickerTemplate" >
27       <input type="color" data-bind="event: { change: change }" />
28   </script>
```

As you can see, we use the `foreach` binding to create a new control for each object in the `UserControls` list that our HTML will be bound to. Inside this, there is a `span` element that is bound to the `IUserControl` interface. Our canvas object will remain unchanged for now, but there are some new elements at the bottom of the page. These new script tags will contain our HTML templates that the user controls will bind to. The button template creates its bindings around the tool selection control interface, binding the text to the `ButtonText` observable and the `click` event to the `Click` function. The color picker only needs to bind the change event to the `Change` method.

The final piece of this is to implement each of our interfaces and bind our view model to the DOM. Each of these types will be placed in separate files in the `Controls` directory. All of the files can be seen in the following screenshot:

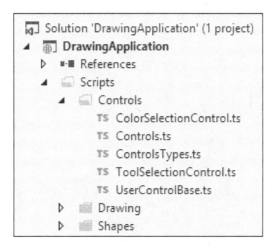

We will start with the base user control object, which will be in the `UserControlBase.ts` file that the remainder of our types will extend:

```
import ControlsTypes = require('Scripts/Controls/ControlsTypes');
class UserControlBase implements ControlsTypes.IUserControl {
    public templateName: string = "TemplateNotProvided";
    constructor(public id: string) {
    }
}
export = UserControlBase;
```

The `id` property comes in as a required property, and therefore will always have a value. The `templateName` string is set to a bad value by default, and this ensures that any type extending the `UserControl` type will be forced to update this property. If an invalid template name is provided, Knockout will generate an error at runtime. However, if an empty string is provided, execution will continue as normal. Now let's provide the implementation for our tool selection buttons:

```
import ControlsTypes = require('Scripts/Controls/ControlsTypes');
import UserControlBase = require('Scripts/Controls/UserControlBase');
import DrawingTypes = require('Scripts/Drawing/DrawingTypes');
class ToolSelectionControl extends UserControlBase
    implements ControlsTypes.IToolSelectionControl {
```

```
    public buttonText: KnockoutObservable<string> = ko.observable("");
    constructor(id: string, public toolType: DrawingTypes.
DrawingToolType,
        public observable: KnockoutObservable<DrawingTypes.
DrawingToolType>) {
        super(id);
        this.templateName = "ButtonTemplate";
        this.buttonText(DrawingTypes.DrawingToolType[this.toolType]);
    }
    public click(viewModel: any, event: JQueryEventObject) {
        this.observable(this.toolType);
    }
}
export = ToolSelectionControl;
```

The overall code here isn't very flashy, but it allows us to add new tool buttons with significantly less effort than what was previously required. The constructor of this type takes in the object's ID to pass to the base type constructor, the `DrawingToolType` value that the object instance will represent, and finally a Knockout observable that will be updated when the button is clicked. Since this is a concrete implementation, we must provide a valid name for our HTML template, and finally, we use a bit of enumeration magic to provide the value for our button's text. The `click` event does nothing more than assign the stored tool type to the observable that was provided when the object was created. The color selection control has an even simpler implementation:

```
import ControlsTypes = require('Scripts/Controls/ControlsTypes');
import UserControlBase = require('Scripts/Controls/UserControlBase');
class ColorSelectionControl extends UserControlBase
    implements ControlsTypes.IColorSelectionControl {
    constructor(id: string, public observable:
KnockoutObservable<string>) {
        super(id);
        this.templateName = "ColorPickerTemplate";
    }
    public change(viewModel: any, event: JQueryEventObject) {
        this.observable((<any>event.currentTarget).value);
    }
}
export = ColorSelectionControl;
```

Creating a ViewModel

Now that we have our reusable controls set up, we need to create the view model that our application will be bound to and make some modifications to our existing types to ensure execution runs smoothly. To maintain the single responsibility pattern, we should create a new model that the UI will be bound to rather than using the `DrawingModel` class, which is responsible for maintaining the state of the shapes in our application. This new model will be bound to the DOM using Knockout and will be responsible for creating and maintaining the state of the application. It will reside in a file called `DrawingModel.ts` inside of the `Drawing` directory. Before we can create this model, we will need to modify the existing drawing model so that our application view model will be able to update the drawing model when the user interacts with the controls. As you can see, in the new interface definition provided, we have made the drawing tool and drawing color properties public members:

```
export interface IDrawingModel {
    selection: IDrawingShape;
    shapes: IDrawingShape[];
    addShape(shape: IDrawingShape);
    getNewShape(location: ShapeTypes.IPoint): IDrawingShape;
    drawingTool: DrawingToolType;
    drawingColor: string;
}
```

The `getDrawingTool` method is no longer necessary because we are providing public access to the underlying instance member. If we were dealing with released software, we would not want to modify this interface directly, but instead extend it and provide a new implementation for the DrawingModel type. However, since this is only a sample application, we can modify it to improve our overall design despite the breaking changes this will cause. Only the internal implementation of this class and a single reference inside of the canvas engine will need to be modified to return our application to a working state. Once these fixes have been made, we can effectively design the application view model that will reside in a file called `DrawingApplicationModel.ts` in the `Scripts` directory:

```
import ControlsTypes = require('Scripts/Controls/ControlsTypes');
import DrawingModel = require('Scripts/Drawing/DrawingModel');
import CanvasEngine = require('Scripts/Drawing/CanvasEngine');
import Controls = require('Scripts/Controls/Controls');
import DrawingTypes = require('Scripts/Drawing/DrawingTypes');

class DrawingApplicationModel {
```

```
    public userControls: KnockoutObservableArray<ControlsTypes.
IUserControl> =
                        ko.observableArray([]);
    public selectedToolType: KnockoutObservable<DrawingTypes.
DrawingToolType> =
                        ko.observable(DrawingTypes.
DrawingToolType.Select);
    public selectedColor: KnockoutObservable<string> =
ko.observable("#000000");
    private _drawingModel: DrawingTypes.IDrawingModel;
    constructor(canvas: HTMLCanvasElement) {
        this._drawingModel = new DrawingModel();
        var engine = new CanvasEngine(canvas, this._drawingModel);
        this._buildControls();
        this._createSubscriptions();
    }
    private _buildControls() {
        var selectionControl = new Controls.ToolSelectionControl("sel
ectButton",
            DrawingTypes.DrawingToolType.Select, this.
selectedToolType);
        var rectangleControl = new Controls.ToolSelectionControl("rec
tangleButton",
            DrawingTypes.DrawingToolType.Rectangle, this.
selectedToolType);
        var lineControl = new Controls.ToolSelectionControl("lineButt
on",
            DrawingTypes.DrawingToolType.Line, this.selectedToolType);
        var colorControl = new Controls.ColorSelectionControl("colorP
icker",
            this.selectedColor);
        this.userControls.push(selectionControl, rectangleControl,
            lineControl, colorControl);
    }
    private _createSubscriptions() {
        this.selectedToolType.subscribe((newValue) => {
            if (this._drawingModel) {
                this._drawingModel.drawingTool = newValue;
            }
        });
```

```
        this.selectedColor.subscribe((newValue) => {
            if (this._drawingModel) {
                this._drawingModel.drawingColor = newValue;
            }
        });
    }
}
export = DrawingApplicationModel;
```

We will need three Knockout observable types: one for the controls we wish to display, another to maintain the currently selected control, and a final one to track the current color. This view model will create and modify the drawing model and canvas engine objects as necessary as well. The constructor takes HTMLCanvasElement, which the engine will use as a parameter and the rest of the application is isolated to within this class. We have two private initialization methods. The first method builds the array of controls that the DOM is bound to. As you can see, we now use code to define these objects rather than manipulate the DOM directly. Each of the tool selection controls receives the observable that the application model uses to track the state of the observable object from the IUpdateObservable interface. The color picker, on the other hand, receives the SelectedColor observable. As you can see, it is now as easy as adding a few lines of code to create a whole new button:

```
var freehandControl = new Controls.ToolSelectionControl("freehandButt
on",
            DrawingTypes.DrawingToolType.Freehand, this.
SelectedToolType);
        this.userControls.push(freehandControl);
```

Once all of these objects are instantiated, they are added to the controls array, causing the Knockout binding to fire and display all of our buttons. This does not get us all the way to the goal, however. The user will be able to interact with each of these controls and their values will be updated in the application model, but the drawing model will have no concept of these changes. The second private method in our application model will bind listeners to the observable values, and any time the value of an observable changes, we will be able to execute some code. In this case, any time the observable maintaining the selected tool changes, we will update the drawing model's DrawingTool property, and any time the selected color changes, we will modify the DrawingColor property.

The entry point into our application, `app.ts`, has now been simplified into just a couple of lines of code that creates the application model and binds it to the DOM:

```
import DrawingApplicationModel = require('Scripts/
DrawingApplicationModel');
$(document).ready(() => {
    var canvas: HTMLCanvasElement =
        <HTMLCanvasElement>window.document.getElementById("drawingCan
vas");
    ko.applyBindings(new DrawingApplicationModel(canvas));
});
```

While the look of our application has not changed at all from the end user's perspective, we have accomplished quite a bit from a development standpoint. Our code has been separated into smaller logical chunks within a nested structure for folder-driven discovery. Adding new user controls requires no direct DOM interaction, and neither does our connection between the DOM and our application model. The unfortunate side effect of this is that it makes the loading of our page inefficient.

Generating a single output file

In the original version of our drawing application, we only had six files to download to the client browser: a single CSS file, our `app.js` file, and the files containing our object types. Each file is a separate web request and all of the files must be loaded before our application can run.

Elements	Network	Sources	Timeline	Profiles	Resources	Audits	Console			
● ⊘ ▽ ≣ ☐ Preserve log ☑ Disable cache										

Name	Method	Status
☐ localhost	GET	200
☐ app.css	GET	200
☐ Enums.js	GET	200
☐ Shapes.js	GET	200
☐ DrawingModel.js	GET	200
☐ CanvasEngine.js	GET	200
☐ app.js	GET	200

This is a relatively speedy process, and on average takes less than 100 ms depending on network latency. However, in our quest to create a large-scale maintainable application, the number of code files we have has exploded. We now have more than 20 files that need to be loaded into the client browser before the application will successfully complete all of its functionality. This has caused our load times to more than double from what they previously were as shown in the following screenshot of the network traffic:

Name	Method	Status
localhost	GET	200
knockout-3.1.0.js	GET	200
app.css	GET	200
jquery-2.1.1.js	GET	200
require.js	GET	200
app.js	GET	200
DrawingApplicationModel.js	GET	200
DrawingModel.js	GET	200
CanvasEngine.js	GET	200
Controls.js	GET	200
DrawingTypes.js	GET	200
Shapes.js	GET	200
ToolSelectionControl.js	GET	200
ColorSelectionControl.js	GET	200
CanvasEngineAction.js	GET	200
DrawingToolType.js	GET	200
DrawingShapes.js	GET	200
UserControlBase.js	GET	200
DrawingShapeBase.js	GET	200
DrawingRectangle.js	GET	200
DrawingLine.js	GET	200

This delay in load time is perfectly acceptable for development purposes (in fact, as we will see in the next chapter, it will actually be preferable). However, if we ever plan to make our application available to consumers, then we will need to reduce the footprint of our JavaScript output. Before implementing AMD modules, this was as simple as providing the compiler with the --out parameter or changing our TypeScript build settings in Visual Studio. However, when the module flag is provided, this is not possible.

To compile all of our resulting JavaScript modules into a single file, we will need at least one more tool at our disposal. Node.js is a fantastic platform that provides a whole host of functionality, and its primary function is to help create scalable network applications. It is available for download from `http://nodejs.org/`. Node provides a ton of functionality, and I encourage you to read through the API documentation and examples to learn more. In our case, we are going to use it as a JavaScript runtime environment. This will allow us to use r.js to trace all of our RequireJS statements and build an optimized module list.

Once we have Node.js installed, we will have access to it from the command line as well as through PowerShell. We will use this in combination with r.js, which was installed in our Visual Studio project when we installed the RequireJS NuGet package. This library is an optimizer for RequireJS and runs in both Node and Rhino.

For more information regarding Rhino, please visit `https://developer.mozilla.org/en-US/docs/Mozilla/Projects/Rhino`.

The optimizer requires a few parameters that will determine how the output is generated. We must provide a name, the path to the resulting output file, a flag that tells the optimizer to search for all of the nested dependencies in our application, and the paths that r.js should look at when performing its optimization. We will place all of these options in a separate JavaScript file that we can modify if we want to change the way we want our final code to be generated:

```
({
    name: "DrawingApplication",
    out: "DrawingApplication.js",
    findNestedDependencies: true,
    optimize: "none",
    paths: {
        'DrawingApplication': 'app'
    }
})
```

As you can see, all of these options are placed on a JSON object that will be provided to the RequireJS optimizer. The one extra flag here is the optimize flag, which determines whether or not the code should be minified.

 For more information about the r.js optimizer, please visit `http://requirejs.org/docs/optimization.html`.

For the sake of readability, we will leave it at none for now. When we actually want to deploy our code, we can simply comment this option out and all of our code will be placed on a single line in a single file. The final thing we must do to generate our optimized JavaScript output file is create a simple PowerShell script that will run the optimizer and provide our options:

```
cls
write-host '-Building Drawing Application'
node Scripts/r.js -o buildSingleFile.js
```

In this script, we clear the current screen, log some output, and finally use Node.js to run the RequireJS optimizer. If everything goes as expected, the optimizer will provide tracing output, letting us know that all of the modules required for our application to work have been included in the optimization. The following screenshot shows the output of running our script and as you can see all of the JavaScript dependencies have been included in the build:

```
Windows PowerShell                                    _  □  X

PS C:\DrawingApplication\DrawingApplication> .\buildApplication.ps1
-Building Drawing Application

Tracing dependencies for: DrawingApplication
Uglifying file: C:/DrawingApplication/DrawingApplication/DrawingApplication.js

C:/DrawingApplication/DrawingApplication/DrawingApplication.js
----------------
C:/DrawingApplication/DrawingApplication/Scripts/Drawing/Enums/CanvasEngineAction.js
C:/DrawingApplication/DrawingApplication/Scripts/Drawing/Enums/DrawingToolType.js
C:/DrawingApplication/DrawingApplication/Scripts/Drawing/DrawingTypes.js
C:/DrawingApplication/DrawingApplication/Scripts/Shapes/Shapes.js
C:/DrawingApplication/DrawingApplication/Scripts/Drawing/DrawingShapes/DrawingShapeBa
se.js
C:/DrawingApplication/DrawingApplication/Scripts/Drawing/DrawingShapes/DrawingRectang
le.js
C:/DrawingApplication/DrawingApplication/Scripts/Drawing/DrawingShapes/DrawingLine.js

C:/DrawingApplication/DrawingApplication/Scripts/Drawing/DrawingShapes/DrawingShapes.
js
C:/DrawingApplication/DrawingApplication/Scripts/Drawing/DrawingModel.js
C:/DrawingApplication/DrawingApplication/Scripts/Drawing/CanvasEngine.js
C:/DrawingApplication/DrawingApplication/Scripts/Controls/UserControlBase.js
C:/DrawingApplication/DrawingApplication/Scripts/Controls/ToolSelectionControl.js
C:/DrawingApplication/DrawingApplication/Scripts/Controls/ColorSelectionControl.js
C:/DrawingApplication/DrawingApplication/Scripts/Controls/Controls.js
C:/DrawingApplication/DrawingApplication/Scripts/DrawingApplicationModel.js
C:/DrawingApplication/DrawingApplication/app.js

PS C:\DrawingApplication\DrawingApplication> _
```

The final piece of this process is modifying our HTML page to point at the resulting output file. Before we can do this, we must understand the output from the PowerShell script we just ran. As we discussed earlier, there are three parameters for AMD modules; however, we only provided two. The module name was left out of the resulting JavaScript for our module definitions, and this caused RequireJS to search the directory structure for modules. Now that we have combined all of these modules into a single file, this is no longer an effective way for us to load modules. Thankfully, the optimizer handles this problem for us:

```
define('DrawingApplication',["require", "exports", 'Scripts/
DrawingApplicationModel'], function(require, exports,
DrawingApplicationModel) {
```

```
$(document).ready(function () {
    var canvas = window.document.getElementById("drawingCanvas");
    ko.applyBindings(new DrawingApplicationModel(canvas));
  });
});
```

This module definition actually represents the output of the app.ts file, which is the entry point to our application. As you can see, the define method is now receiving all three parameters. Based on the parameters we provided to the optimizer, the name given for the app module is now DrawingApplication. RequireJS will take note of this name, and anywhere another module requires it, it will be loaded instantly rather than searching the file structure for a JavaScript file with the given pathname and filename. The last thing we must do is modify our HTML page to point at the new single output file. This is done by setting the data-main attribute for the RequireJS tag to the newly built JavaScript file as shown in the following screenshot:

```
index.html  ⊕  ✕
 1    <!DOCTYPE html>
 2    <html lang="en">
 3    <head>
 4        <meta charset="utf-8" />
 5        <title>TypeScript HTML App</title>
 6        <link rel="stylesheet" href="app.css" type="text/css" />
 7        <script src="Scripts/jquery-2.1.1.js" ></script>
 8        <script src="Scripts/knockout-3.1.0.js"></script>
 9        <script data-main="DrawingApplication" src="Scripts/require.js"></script>
10    </head>
```

We only need to modify the data-main attribute of the script tag we use to load RequireJS and it will handle the rest. RequireJS will see that it does not have a definition for DrawingApplication and will search the filesystem relative to the location of require.js for DrawingApplication.js and load it.

This behavior can be modified through the require.config method. For more information about require.config, please visit http://requirejs.org/docs/api.html#config.

This will cause all of our module definitions to be evaluated and an entry will be created for each one by RequireJS for instantaneous loading when they are required. Finally, when RequireJS reaches the DrawingApplication module, which has been placed last in the resulting output file to ensure all of its dependencies have been defined, it will be defined and then the function will run.

The `DrawingApplicationModel` class, which has already been defined, will be found in the RequireJS cache and will not be dependent on loading another JavaScript file. As you can see, the loading of our application code is now only a single web request, which will significantly decrease the application load time:

Q Elements Network Sources Timeline Profiles Resources Audits Console		
● ⊘ ▽ ▤ ▢ Preserve log ☑ Disable cache		
Name	Method	Status
☐ index.html	GET	200
☐ app.css	GET	200
☐ jquery-2.1.1.js	GET	200
☐ knockout-3.1.0.js	GET	200
☐ require.js	GET	200
☐ DrawingApplication.js	GET	200

Now, we can keep our code separated in individual code files and not have to worry about performance in production. In the next chapter, when we cover debugging, this will become even more important for aiding our development of application-scale JavaScript projects.

Styling the application

So far, we have only covered the way we develop the source code for our applications. However, styling the application is just as important as the functionality. The code that we write can be completely free of bugs, but if the appearance and feel of the application is poor, users will not adopt it. Traditionally, when developing web applications using HTML pages, we would use **Cascading Style Sheets (CSS)** to style our objects. However, similar to the way TypeScript improves JavaScript development, a language called LESS has been developed that will compile into plain CSS. LESS is available for standalone download from `http://lesscss.org/`, or in the case of Visual Studio, it can be installed with Mads Kristensen's Web Essentials plugin. This plugin is available through the Extensions and Updates window just like the NuGet Package Manager was.

Web Essentials 2013 for Update 2
Adds many useful features to Visual Studio for web developers. Requires VS2013 Update 2 RTM

Once this has been installed, we can add a LESS style sheet to our application. LESS has a lot of incredibly useful features that will help us create a friendly user interface in a more robust manner. We have the ability to declare variables and nest styles within each other. Let's use LESS to improve the feel of our application. Currently, a user has no visual cues informing them what tool they are currently working with. We could use some code to change the cursor type when a button is clicked; however, this can be overridden by other elements on the page, including the `CanvasEngine` class that our application relies on. Instead, we will use Knockout bindings combined with generated CSS styles. First, we will need to create a new property on the `IToolSelectionControl` interface and the `ToolSelectionControl` class to store whether or not the current control is selected or not:

```
import ControlsTypes = require('Scripts/Controls/ControlsTypes');
import UserControlBase = require('Scripts/Controls/UserControlBase');
import DrawingTypes = require('Scripts/Drawing/DrawingTypes');
class ToolSelectionControl extends UserControlBase
    implements ControlsTypes.IToolSelectionControl {
    public buttonText: KnockoutObservable<string> = ko.observable("");
    public isSelected: KnockoutComputed<boolean> = null;
    constructor(id: string, public toolType: DrawingTypes.
DrawingToolType,
        public observable: KnockoutObservable<DrawingTypes.
DrawingToolType>) {
        super(id);
        this.templateName = "ButtonTemplate";
        this.buttonText(DrawingTypes.DrawingToolType[this.toolType]);
        this.isSelected = ko.computed(() => {
            return this.observable() == this.toolType;
        });
    }
    public click(viewModel: any, event: JQueryEventObject) {
        this.observable(this.toolType);
    }
}
export = ToolSelectionControl;
```

As you can see, we created a new `KnockoutComputed` object that will return a Boolean and that our HTML will be bound to. Instead of storing an instance value like observables do, computed objects run a function that is responsible for either setting or returning the value. In this case, we check whether the value of the observable the control is supposed to update is the same as the tool that this control is associated with. If they are the same, then a true value will be returned; otherwise, the result will be false. By including another observable object within the body of this function, Knockout will create a subscription to this object, and any time its value is changed, this function will be re-evaluated. This keeps us from having to write any additional logic to update an observable whenever one of these controls is clicked. Binding to computed objects is the same as binding to observables as they share a common super class.

```html
<script type="text/html" id="ButtonTemplate">
    <button class="tool-select-button" data-bind="text: buttonText, click: click,
            css: { 'selected': isSelected }" />
</script>
```

In the preceding screenshot, you can see we have added a class to our button that we will be able to provide styles for and then the additional Knockout binding. This binding will add the `'selected'` class to the button element if the computed object returns a true value. Now we need to define these styles and include them in our application. One of the most valuable features of LESS is the ability to define variables that can be reused through all of your LESS files. In the following example, we define several colors that we want to use throughout our application:

```less
@selectionColor: #1111DD;
@accentColor: white;
@borderColor: black;
```

The `selectionColor` variable will be used to denote the color of the tool that is currently selected, while the `accentColor` and `borderColor` variables will be used for a variety of purposes. Rather than explicitly defining these colors for each style and having to change every place they are used, we will simply be able to change the value of these variables and the entire look of our application can change. To use these variables, we simply import the `.less` file that contains them and they will be available:

```less
@import 'ApplicationColors.less';
```

```less
.tool-select-button {
    background-color: @accentColor;
    border-color: @borderColor;
    &.selected {
        background-color: @selectionColor;
        color: @accentColor;
    }
}
input[type=color] {
    border-color: @borderColor;
}
canvas {
    border: 4px solid @borderColor;
}
```

We use our variables to define the values that our styles will have. The buttons that now have the `.tool-select-button` class will be given new background and border colors. There is also a nested style shown, which when compiled into CSS will create another style that represents the union between these two styles. The final style puts a border around the color picker. When the LESS code is compiled, the resulting CSS will look similar to the following code:

```css
.tool-select-button {
  background-color: #ffffff;
  border-color: #000000;
}
.tool-select-button.selected {
  background-color: #1111dd;
  color: #ffffff;
}
input[type=color] {
  border-color: #000000;
}
canvas {
  border: 4px solid #000000;
}
```

Notice that all of the variables have been removed and replaced with the values they represent. LESS variables have no representation in CSS, so they behave similar to interfaces in TypeScript in that they have no compiled output. If a LESS file is imported that does contain styles, all of those styles will be included in the resulting CSS file as a merged set of styles. Now we can simply modify our HTML to link our style sheet and our application will have a better user experience.

```html
index.html
1    <!DOCTYPE html>
2    <html lang="en">
3    <head>
4        <meta charset="utf-8" />
5        <title>TypeScript HTML App</title>
6        <link rel="stylesheet" href="app.css" type="text/css" />
7        <link rel="stylesheet" href="DrawingApplication.css" type="text/css" />
8        <script src="Scripts/jquery-2.1.1.js" ></script>
9        <script src="Scripts/knockout-3.1.0.js"></script>
10       <script data-main="app" src="Scripts/require.js"></script>
11   </head>
12   <body>
13       <h1>Drawing Application</h1>
14       <div id="content">
15           <div data-bind="foreach: userControls">
16               <span data-bind="attr: { id: id }, template: { name: templateName }"></span>
17           </div>
18           <canvas id="drawingCanvas" height="400" width="570" />
19       </div>
20   </body>
21   </html>
```

When we run the application, the **Select** button will display the selected style because the KnockoutComputed object we added evaluated to true for that control. Selecting any of the other tools will cause the bindings to be re-evaluated and the styles to change with the user action. Any of the elements with a border on them have a consistent color, and if we ever want to modify that, we will only have to change it in a single location. This will save us a significant amount of time if we ever need to restyle the application.

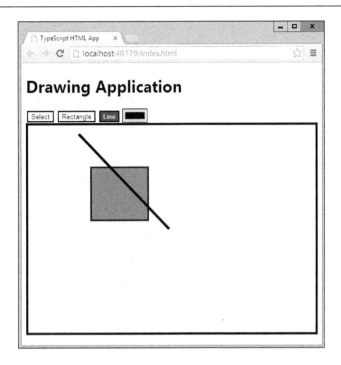

Summary

In this chapter, we have covered several ways to improve the way we develop and deploy enterprise-level JavaScript applications. We converted the drawing application to AMD modules to eliminate the need for manually managing how scripts are loaded. We created bindings between our HTML and TypeScript code using Knockout, which allow us to easily extend the behavior of our application with minimal effort. Then, we looked to improve the speed at which our application is available by reducing all of our modules into a single optimized JavaScript file. Finally, we added LESS style sheets that allowed us to create a robust set of styles that could be easily maintained and modified. In the next chapter, we will look at the different methods used to debug TypeScsript as well as how we can provide unit tests for our application.

Debugging TypeScript

8

We have covered all the skills you will need to write large-scale applications using TypeScript. The compiler and language constructs provided by TypeScript allow us to quickly and safely develop reliable programs. As all experienced developers know though, code that compiles doesn't always perform as expected. In this chapter, we will discuss the different options available to debug TypeScript once it is deployed and running. We will also cover unit testing, which will allow us to test the functionality with code. In this chapter, we will investigate the following topics:

- Debugging
- Test-driven development

Debugging

When developing plain old JavaScript applications, our debugging options are usually dependent upon the available tooling in each browser. Most modern browsers include some form of developer console that allows us to view the scripts running on a web page. From this console, we can set breakpoints and investigate the behavior of our application. We can perform the same task in TypeScript applications; however, this leaves us stepping through the generated JavaScript rather than the TypeScript code we actually wrote.

Source maps

As we discussed earlier, source maps are a way to map one code file, generally minified, back to the original code file. In TypeScript, this concept holds true and allows us to step through our non-compiled TypeScript code. To enable this functionality, the first thing we must do is ensure that our project settings are set to generate source maps; this setting is on by default:

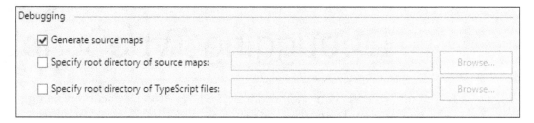

This setting will provide the `--sourcemap` parameter to the compiler and allow us to link the output JavaScript file to the original TypeScript file. In most modern browsers, this will cause the TypeScript file to download to the client and we will be able to set breakpoints and step through our code line by line.

Debuggers

There are several ways to debug our application's code, and it is likely that we will need a combination of them to ensure we provide a high quality application. Modern browsers such as Chrome, Firefox, and Internet Explorer all include a developer console that provides debugging features for web applications. In the following screenshot, you can see that we can step directly into our TypeScript code using the Chrome developer tools:

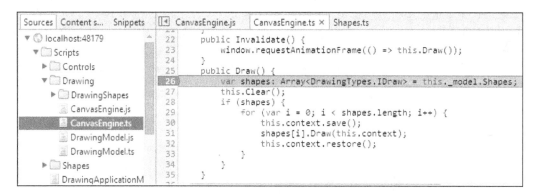

Here, you can see that we have set a breakpoint on the `Draw` method of the `CanvasEngine` of our drawing application. In the source window, both the JavaScript file and the TypeScript file are visible, as are the type annotations we included in the TypeScript file. This is an incredibly powerful feature for developers because it prevents us from having to translate the generated JavaScript code back to a particular line of the original TypeScript code. With Visual Studio and Internet Explorer, we are actually able to debug directly from the IDE. This enables us to use all of the tools and features available in Visual Studio in the same way that we could debug C# code. This includes the call stack, adding any watch expressions, as well as object exploration, as you can see in the following screenshot:

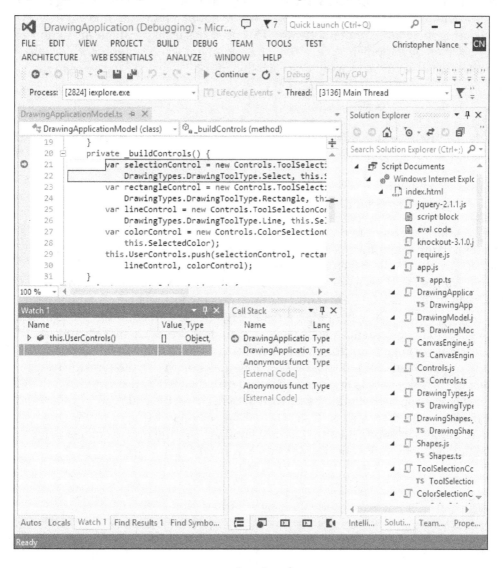

It is important to test our application's code in all of the environments that it is expected to run in. Each browser implements its own JavaScript engine and has adopted different sets of features from the HTML5 standard. Being familiar with each of the different developer consoles will be important to track down and resolve issues that may not be readily apparent in another browser.

Test-driven development

As our applications grow in both size and complexity, it is more important than ever for us to deliver software with as few bugs as possible. Manual testing is inconsistent and slow, which means we need to adopt a more methodical way of ensuring the quality of our software. This need has brought about the notion of test-driven development. Test-driven development is a development cycle that repeats a small set of steps to ensure each line of code is tested. The steps in the test-driven development life cycle are:

- Adding a test
- Running the tests
- Writing the code
- Running the tests again
- Refactoring the code

The first thing we want to do is write a test to verify some functionality. This creates a requirement for the code that we have yet to write. This test will initially fail when writing unit tests for new functionality; this is expected and helps to verify that the test does have a failure state. At this point, we run all of the tests, verifying that preexisting tests still pass and our new test fails. If the new test does not fail, the functionality has either already been implemented or the test is invalid and needs to be rewritten. Once we have a valid test, we must implement the feature that we are attempting to test. This code does not have to be perfect upon the first implementation; the goal is only to write enough code to pass the test. When the functionality is implemented, we rerun the tests and verify that our code is effective. If not, then it must be corrected. Otherwise, the code can be refactored; but the test must always pass. This process is repeated until every feature has tests and an implementation. Now that we are familiar with the process of test-driven development, let's look at how unit testing works in TypeScript.

For more information about test-driven development, please visit `http://msdn.microsoft.com/en-us/library/aa730844(v=vs.80).aspx`.

Unit testing

Unit tests are code blocks that test small units of functionality with a set of control data and expected results. These tests are reliable and reusable, ensuring that our code is not only tested for the current version of the application, but for all future releases. This will ensure that any added or modified features do not break existing functionality and will alert us of a problem well ahead of time. TypeScript does not come with any built-in unit testing tools; however, the web community once again filled this hole. A unit test framework has been created by Maxim Fridberg and gives you a simple way to create and view all of your unit tests for libraries that you have created. The name of the framework is MaxUnit and is available for download from `https://github.com/KnowledgeLakegithub/MaxUnit`, or it is available as a NuGet package called `KL.Testing.MaxUnit`.

Created by: KnowledgeLake

Id: KL.Testing.MaxUnit

Version: 1.0.0.14

Last Published: 7/30/2014

Downloads: 0

Report Abuse

Description:

Typescript Testing Framework with Requirejs Isolation

Tags: KnowledgeLake

Dependencies:

> jquery.TypeScript.DefinitelyTyped (≥ 0.8.1)
> knockout.TypeScript.DefinitelyTyped (≥ 0.5.0)
> requirejs.TypeScript.DefinitelyTyped (≥ 0.1.7)

Each item above may have sub-dependencies subject to additional license agreements.

This package will add a number of files to our Visual Studio project including sample usage of the framework. The advantage of MaxUnit is that it allows us to write tests in TypeScript for our TypeScript libraries. There are a number of other testing frameworks available to test JavaScript libraries, including Jasmine (https://github.com/pivotal/jasmine/) and QUnit (http://qunitjs.com/). It is generally best to keep your test code separate from the implementation code, to ensure that it will be tested in the same manner that it will be used. To get a feel for how unit testing works, let's take the Shapes library that we created for the drawing application and create a series of tests to ensure proper functionality. The Shapes library outputs to a single JavaScript file and has interfaces associated with it that we can use to test our code.

Adding tests

Now that we have the tooling installed, let's begin the process of unit testing our library. The first thing we need to do is add the Shapes library to the testing project. This process can be done manually or can be automated using PowerShell to deploy the latest version of our code. For now, we will handle it manually so that we can focus on testing. Once our library is added to the project, we can begin writing tests. We will create a separate testing class to test each of our objects in the Shapes library. Let's start with the simplest class in the library, the Point class, to get a feel for testing. In the following sample, you can see we have created a new class called test_Point that contains all of our tests for this particular class:

```
/// <reference path="../../maxunit.ts" />
/// <reference path="../../scripts/typings/shapes/shapestypes.d.ts" />
class test_Point extends maxUnit.TestClassBase {
    private _shapes: Shapes = null;
    constructor() {
        //give test suite a name
        super('test_Point');
        //add test by name
    }
    setUpAsync(dfdSetup: JQueryDeferred<any>) {
        var cb = super.setUpAsync;
        require(['/Scripts/Shapes/Shapes.js'], (Shapes) => {
            this._shapes = Shapes;
            cb(dfdSetup);
        });
    }
    tearDown() {
```

```
            super.tearDown();
        }
    }

    export = test_Point;
```

The class inherits from the `maxUnit` base class `TestClassBase`, which provides methods used to register tests with the testing framework. The constructor calls the base constructor and provides the name for this set of tests. Eventually, this section will also contain the registration for each of our unit tests. The `setUpAsync` method will be used to set up any necessary mock objects and create a reference to the `Shapes` library. If our library contained jQuery or any other dependencies, we would mock these objects to ensure our library performs as expected. The `teardown` method provides a place to provide any cleanup logic that you may want to execute after the tests have run. Now, let's begin by writing some very simple tests that will verify the creation of a `Point` object. Each unit test should be arranged into three sections:

- Arrange
- Act
- Assert

The arrange section will create any objects we need to perform our test, act will perform the operations that make up our test, and assert will verify the results of these operations. In the following tests, you can see that we provide implementations for all three sections of the test to verify the initialization of the x and y members of the `Point` class:

```
    test_PointInitX() {
        //Arrange
        var p: IPoint = new this._shapes.Point(3, 4);
        //Act
        var x = p.x;
        //Assert
        this.Assert.AreIdentical(3, x, "Should return 3");
    }
    test_PointInitY() {
        //Arrange
        var p: IPoint = new this._shapes.Point(3, 4);
        //Act
        var y = p.y;
        //Assert
        this.Assert.AreIdentical(4, y, "Should return 4");
    }
```

As you can see, we create a new `Point` object during the arrange phase of our tests. We then evaluate the properties of the `Point` object during the act phase, and finally we assert whether or not the object was initialized correctly. Before we can run these tests though, we must add them to the `Tests` array that is provided by `TestClassBase`:

```
constructor() {
    //give test suite a name
    super('test_Point');
    //add test by name
    this.AddTest('test_PointInitX', 'Test Point.x value init');
    this.AddTest('test_PointInitY', 'Test Point.y value init');
}
```

Finally, we must add our test class to the list of test classes defined in the `tests.js` file provided by MaxUnit. This will ensure that our test class gets registered with the testing framework and that all of our tests will be run upon execution:

```
define(function () {
  //add test modules relative to /tests
  return ["ShapeTests/test_Point"];
});
```

That's all we have to do to write unit tests for TypeScript code. If we set the testing project as the start-up project for our Visual Studio solution and run it with MaxUnit, the UI will display a list of all tests that have been run and their result, as shown in the following screenshot:

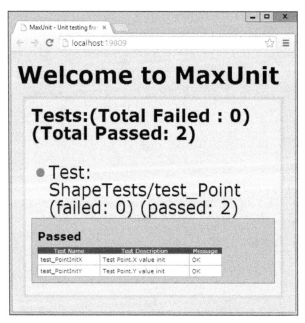

These are both very simple tests that cover the most basic path used to create `Point` objects; however, when writing unit tests, we want to cover as many scenarios as possible to verify proper functionality. For instance, rather than just testing specific classes, let's write some tests around an interface, which will create a series of tests that can be successfully run on multiple concrete implementations. In the following example, you can see we have created a new set of tests that will be used to test the `IRectangle` interface:

```
/// <reference path="../../maxunit.ts" />
/// <reference path="../../scripts/typings/shapes/shapestypes.d.ts" />
class test_IRectangle extends maxUnit.TestClassBase {
    private _shapes: Shapes = null;
    constructor() {
        //give test suite a name
        super('test_Point');
        //add test by name
        this.AddTest('test_RectangleResize', 'Test resizing of
Rectangle');
    }
    setUpAsync(dfdSetup: JQueryDeferred<any>) {
        var cb = super.setUpAsync;

        require(['/Scripts/Shapes/Shapes.js'], (Shapes) => {
            this._shapes = Shapes;
            cb(dfdSetup);
        });
    }
    tearDown() {
        super.tearDown();
    }
    test_RectangleResize() {
        //Arrange
        var rect: IRectangle = new this._shapes.Rectangle(4, 6);
        this.test_IRectangleResize(rect);
    }
    test_IRectangleResize(r: IRectangle) {
        //Act
        r.resize(3, 9);
        //Assert
        this.Assert.AreIdentical(9, r.width, "Should return 9");
    }
}

export = test_IRectangle;
```

As you can see, our class structure is very similar; however, the pieces of the unit test have been separated into two logical parts. The first is the creation of the object we are attempting to test, and the second is the interface that we will be testing. The second piece of this test can be reused again and again for each class we create that implements IRectangle. For instance, squares are quite similar to rectangles; in fact, we could implement them in such a way that they have the exact same set of properties. We can very easily add a new class to our Shapes library that will represent squares:

```
export class Square implements IRectangle {
    constructor(public height: number, public width) {
        this.width = this.height;
    }
    public resize(height: number, width: number) {
        this.height = height;
        this.width = height;
    }
}
```

As you can see, this class upholds both the IRectangle interface and the notion of squares by making sure that the width and height properties get set to the same value. We can now write a third testing method in the test_IRectangle class that will instantiate a new Square object and run it through the resize test that is being used for the Rectangle objects:

```
test_SquareResize() {
        //Arrange
        var square: IRectangle = new this._shapes.Square(4, 6);
        this.test_IRectangleResize(square);
}
```

By using our interface abstraction, our tests become reusable units of code for multiple object types. Running these tests together results in the following output:

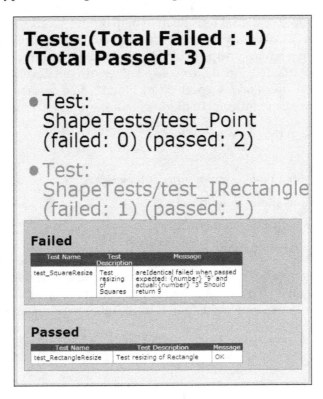

The square test has failed. The interface was implemented so our code was able to compile; however, this has exposed a problem with our assumption about squares. Through our implementation, we forced the behavior of a square onto an `IRectangle` type. This test exposed the fact that we broke the Liskov substitution principle that we discussed in *Chapter 4, Object-oriented Programming with TypeScript*. We are not able to safely substitute one `IRectangle` object for another, which could result in unexpected behavior.

Summary

In this chapter, we discussed the final pieces of TypeScript development. We discussed source maps and how TypeScript uses them to map output JavaScript files back to the original TypeScript file, allowing us to step through our code before compilation. We looked at the different environments in which we could debug our code, whether it be in the browser or the IDE. Finally, we looked at test-driven development and how it allows us to catch errors and unexpected functionality in a reusable and consistent manner. We discussed a large number of topics in a short period of time:

- Working with the compiler
- TypeScript's language constructs
- Object-oriented development with TypeScript
- Asynchronous module definitions
- Integrating with external libraries
- Test-driven development

We built a drawing application using each of these different topics and refined it as our needs changed and knowledge increased. You are now capable of starting a new application in TypeScript and taking it from initial requirements to a polished final product.

Index

G

generic objects 42-44

H

Hello World
about 9
build options 14, 15
command-line compilation 10-12
new project, creating 13
Visual Studio, integrating 12

I

IAdder interface 24
IBounds interface 34
ICalculator interface 24
IDE
setting up 9
inheritance 64-68
instance members 28-31
interfaces
about 23-27
IAdder interface 24
ICalculator interface 24
inheritance 23
instance members 28-31
ISubtractor interface 24
properties 31-34
static members 28-31
Interface Segregation Principle
about 63
URL 63
internal modules 37-42
ISubtractor interface 24

J

Jasmine
URL 156
JavaScript closures and module pattern
URL 26
JavaScript output 51-53
jQuery
integrating with 109-112
URL 112

K

Knockout
integrating with 112-114

L

LESS
URL 144
Liskov Substitution Principle
about 63
URL 63

M

MaxUnit
URL 155
method overloading 72
method overrides 75, 76
Model View Controller (MVC) 130
Model View ViewModel (MVVM) 130
modules
about 37
external modules 37
internal modules 37
mouse events, drawing application 94-97

N

new project
creating 13
Node.js
URL 140
Notepad++
URL 8
NuGet packages
installing 107-109

O

object-oriented design
URL 76
Object-oriented Programming. *See* OOP
objects 62
object types 19
OOP
about 61
URL 76

Open/Closed Principle
about 63
URL 63
operator overloading 73-75

P

polymorphism
about 72
method overloading 72
method overrides 75, 76
operator overloading 73-75
primitive types 18
project
setting up 79-81
properties 31-34

Q

QUnit
URL 156

R

require.config
URL 143
RequireJS
API and configuration files, URL 124
URL 119
using 115-119
Rhino
URL 141
r.js optimizer
URL 141

S

setUpAsync method 157
shapes
about 82
basic shapes 82-84
drawing 84-89
single output file
generating 138-144
Single Responsibility Principle
about 63
URL 63

SOLID 63
source maps
about 54-56
generating 152
static members 28-31

T

teardown method 157
test-driven development
about 154
steps 154
tests, adding 156-161
unit testing 155, 156
URL 155
tests
adding 156-161
third-party library integration
about 107
NuGet packages, installing 107-109
RequireJS used 115-119
with jQuery 109-112
with Knockout 112, 113
type parameters 19
types, TypeScript
about 18, 19
Any type 18
object type 19
primitive type 18
TypeScript
about 5, 6
advanced options 56-60
advantages 6-8
classes 25
enums 34
functions 20-22
generic objects 42-44
interfaces 23-27
modules 37
primitive types 19
types 18
URL 8
TypeScript compiler
advanced options 56-60
JavaScript output 51-53
source maps 54-56

U

unit test
  about 155, 156
  act section 157
  arrange section 157
  assert section 157
user controls
  binding 130
  reusable controls 130-134
user options, drawing application 97-103

V

ViewModel
  creating 135-137
Visual Studio
  integrating 12
  URL 12

Thank you for buying
TypeScript Essentials

About Packt Publishing

Packt, pronounced 'packed', published its first book "*Mastering phpMyAdmin for Effective MySQL Management*" in April 2004 and subsequently continued to specialize in publishing highly focused books on specific technologies and solutions.

Our books and publications share the experiences of your fellow IT professionals in adapting and customizing today's systems, applications, and frameworks. Our solution based books give you the knowledge and power to customize the software and technologies you're using to get the job done. Packt books are more specific and less general than the IT books you have seen in the past. Our unique business model allows us to bring you more focused information, giving you more of what you need to know, and less of what you don't.

Packt is a modern, yet unique publishing company, which focuses on producing quality, cutting-edge books for communities of developers, administrators, and newbies alike. For more information, please visit our website: www.packtpub.com.

About Packt Open Source

In 2010, Packt launched two new brands, Packt Open Source and Packt Enterprise, in order to continue its focus on specialization. This book is part of the Packt Open Source brand, home to books published on software built around Open Source licenses, and offering information to anybody from advanced developers to budding web designers. The Open Source brand also runs Packt's Open Source Royalty Scheme, by which Packt gives a royalty to each Open Source project about whose software a book is sold.

Writing for Packt

We welcome all inquiries from people who are interested in authoring. Book proposals should be sent to author@packtpub.com. If your book idea is still at an early stage and you would like to discuss it first before writing a formal book proposal, contact us; one of our commissioning editors will get in touch with you.

We're not just looking for published authors; if you have strong technical skills but no writing experience, our experienced editors can help you develop a writing career, or simply get some additional reward for your expertise.

AngularJS Web Application Development Blueprints

ISBN: 978-1-78328-561-7   Paperback: 300 pages

A practical guide to developing powerful web applications with AngularJS

1. Get to grips with AngularJS and the development of single-page web applications.

2. Develop rapid prototypes with ease using Bootstraps Grid system.

3. Complete and in depth tutorials covering many applications.

ReSharper Essentials

ISBN: 978-1-84969-870-2   Paperback: 124 pages

Make your Microsoft Visual Studio work smarter with ReSharper

1. Discover the most useful features of ReSharper and how to implement them effectively.

2. Find out what is wrong with your code and use quick fixes to eliminate errors and code smells.

3. A practical guide to ReSharper 8.1 focused on teaching you the most intuitive shortcuts.

Please check **www.PacktPub.com** for information on our titles

TYPO3 Templates

ISBN: 978-1-84719-840-2   Paperback: 328 pages

Create and modify templates with TypoScript
and TemplaVoila

1. Build dynamic and powerful TYPO3
   templates using TypoScript, TemplaVoila,
   and other core technologies.

2. Customize dynamic menus, logos, and
   headers using tricks you won't find in
   the official documentation.

3. Build content elements and template extensions
   to overhaul and improve TYPO3's default
   backend editing experience.

TYPO3 4.2 E-Commerce

ISBN: 978-1-84719-852-5   Paperback: 212 pages

Design, build, and profit from a sophisticated
feature-rich online store using TYPO3

1. Run your business like a pro and earn good
   profits in your online shop by harnessing all
   the features of TYPO 3.

2. Create an effective search system for productive
   navigation of your site.

3. Incorporate smart payment and
   delivery modules.

4. Packed with expert guidance on all aspects
   of building a lucrative online shop.

Please check **www.PacktPub.com** for information on our titles

www.ingramcontent.com/pod-product-compliance
Lightning Source LLC
LaVergne TN
LVHW081343050326
832903LV00024B/1281